how to build a
PATIO, PORCH
and SUNDECK

Donald R. Brann

FIRST PRINTING — 1979

Published by
DIRECTIONS SIMPLIFIED, INC.

Division of
EASI-BILD PATTERN CO., INC.
Briarcliff Manor, NY 10510

Library of Congress Card No. 78-55238

FIRST PRINTING — 1979

GET SMART ...
or get clobbered

We live in a fast changing world where ripoff has become a national pastime. It's a game the quick buck artist, gyp garage repair shop, even a President plays when he grants "loans" to countries who never repay. Ripoff plagues every section of society and it's especially prevalent when it comes to home improvement.

Today's rules call for charging the customer whatever he can be conned into paying, not how much skill, time, labor or material the work requires. Economic survival and the way you live depend on how you invest spare time doing what needs to be done. Every hour you transform into building labor, every dollar you invest in material, not only adds comfort and convenience, but also a long term Capital Gains.

This book assumes you have never built a patio, porch, sundeck, or enclosed an existing porch. In non-technical words and pictures, it explains every step. Directions first simplify building a patio with an Easi-Bild engineered air vent. Instead of roofing over and trapping a lot of hot air as with most patios, the vented roof assures a free flow of air. This helps cool, instead of heat, adjacent rooms. Directions also explain how to screen in a patio, build a porch or enclose an existing one.

Doing something today you didn't know how to do yesterday is life's way of keeping you young. Those who say, "I can't," before they say, "I'll try," grow old long before they've begun to live. Welcome every opportunity to expand your sphere of activity and see how much more living you get out of life.

Don R. Brann

TABLE OF CONTENTS

12 — Tools
13 — How to Build a Patio
14 — Site Selection
19 — Building Permit
20 — How to Lay Out Guide Lines
27 — Slab on Grade
35 — Footings for Concrete Block
40 — Framing a Patio
49 — Vent Rafters
56 — How to Change Angle of Rafter
60 — How to Install an Outside Door
63 — Building Steps
64 — How to Screen a Patio
65 — Wood Screens
69 — Aluminum Screens
74 — How to Build a Porch or Carport
     with Sundeck Above
85 — Porch on Posts
93 — Stair Building
100 — Construction Against Block
      and Brick Houses
102 — How to Enclose a Porch
112 — Installing Insulation
114 — Installing Ceilings, Paneling
115 — Casement Window Trim
117 — Siding Simplified
123 — The Exposed Porch Rafter
124 — Gutter and Leader Installation
126 — Privacy Partition
133 — Facts About Glazing Windows
138 — Repairing Lawn Furniture
140 — Cross Reference
      to Other Books and Patterns

HOW TO SAVE A BUNDLE

Since even a new house and equipment frequently require costly repair, homeowners represent a lush market for fast talking patio, porch, roofing and siding salesmen. Don't let these characters "con" you into thinking there's any great mystery to making these improvements. Substantial savings can be effected on even the smallest job when you shop for material and labor. When you know what materials are needed, where and when each piece of lumber is installed, you begin to think, talk and act like a "pro." This enables you to shop for labor as intelligently as you shop for material. The savings can be terrific. As a bonus, you get a far better job.

This book not only explains how to build a 12 x 20' patio that can double as a carport, but also construction of a raised porch and sundeck. Directions explain how to screen a patio; how to replace square and round porch columns or transform an existing porch into enclosed living space; how to build a flat roofed porch with a second story sundeck.

Those who have had it with the neighbors' dogs or children will find a solution to a difficult problem when they build a privacy partition. This can double as a swimming pool enclosure, note page 126.

Step by step directions also explain how to apply vinyl, aluminum and hardboard siding, install leaders and gutters, how to remove a window to install a door or sliding glass doors. Reglazing wood and metal windows is also explained in easy to follow directions.

Read this book slowly, not once, but two or three times. Note location of each part in each illustration when same is mentioned. Obtain a permit where required.

PATIO

SUNDECK

PRIVACY PARTITION

THE BACK PORCH

9

ENCLOSED PORCH

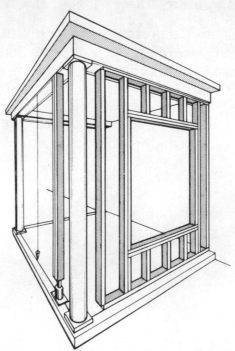

By following procedure outlined, you can build a patio or porch to size specified or to any size required. Study each illustration when text mentions same. This helps visualize construction. If any step isn't completely clear, ask your lumber dealer to explain. Actual construction is simplified when a piece of lumber becomes a sill, stud, post, rafter, etc. Learning what goes where and when creates confidence. It also permits intelligently shopping for material and labor.

If you decide to hire help for full or part time work, take the offensive. Make certain they want and need the work and are willing to give you an honest day's work for the wages you are willing and able to offer. Be sure to spell out how many hours of work you expect for a day's pay. Working alongside a skilled mason or carpenter not only gets the job done faster, but also provides valuable experience. If you employ any help, even a neighbor's son or daughter, ask your insurance agent to temporarily cover their services. Giving youth a chance to learn any of the building trades can help shape their future, while it provides the assistance you need mixing and pouring concrete, lifting frames, etc.

Building is fun and a great way to enjoy peace of mind. It provides healthy exercise, relaxation, a feeling of accomplishment, while it opens your eyes to new fields of endeavor. But remember, work only when you feel like it, and only for as long as you feel physically fit. Once you become tired, accidents and errors occur. Don't overtax your physical capability. Always get help.

This book covers important, money saving and money making improvements. What you do to your home can be done to others. This enables you to start a business with only an investment of tools and materials.

TOOLS NEEDED

The tools shown in Illus. 1 are those needed to build the improvements offered in this book. They consist of a pick and shovel, mason's hoe, carpenter and line levels, square, hammer, brace and bits, crosscut and rip saws, steel measuring tape, folding rule, screwdriver, chisels, building line, etc. Since you can save half or more of the contract cost building, or helping to build each project, invest part of these savings in the purchase of a radial arm saw or circular saw. These save so much time and labor, it's like having the help of a skilled carpenter at no extra cost. Operation of electric tools has been so simplified, anyone who follows directions provided has no difficulty using them in a professional manner.

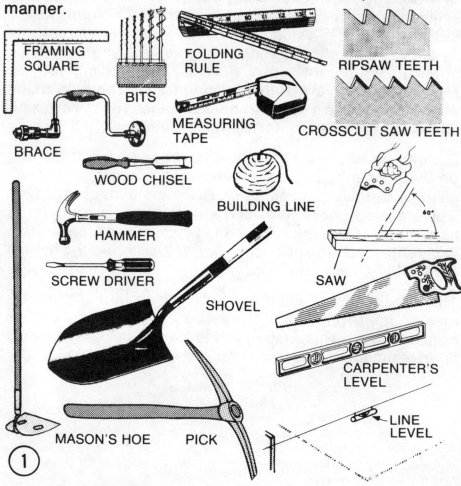

FRAMING SQUARE

BITS

FOLDING RULE

RIPSAW TEETH

BRACE

MEASURING TAPE

CROSSCUT SAW TEETH

WOOD CHISEL

BUILDING LINE

60°

HAMMER

SCREW DRIVER

SHOVEL

SAW

CARPENTER'S LEVEL

LINE LEVEL

MASON'S HOE   PICK

1

HOW TO BUILD A PATIO

Step by step directions explain how to build a patio 12' deep by 20' long. Any other size can be constructed by following procedure outlined.

LIST OF MATERIALS FOR A 12 x 20' PATIO

This list specifies material required for a patio with an engineered air vent. When ordering lumber, state size (4 x 4), number of pieces (3), length (8'). For example: 4 x 4 - 3/8'.

LUMBER

4 x 4 — 3/8' posts
2 x 6 — 8/12' rafters
2 x 6 — 2/20 or 2/10, 1/8, 1/12' plate
2 x 4 — 1/12' vent rafters
2 x 4 — 4/10', 1/14' cats

5/4 x 6 — 1/20 or 2/10' fascia
1 x 10 — 1/20 or 2/10' ridge
1 x 4 — 1/4' vent fascia
1 x 3 — 2/12' rafter fascia
1 x 2 — 1/10, 1/12' vent

ROOFING

7 — 33½'' x 14' fiber glass panels*
40' redwood filler strip (fascia and vent screens)
20' flashing to match roofing panels
2 boxes 1¾'' aluminum nails with neoprene washers
Sealing cord of non-drying calking
Clear mastic

HARDWARE

6 — ¼ x 2'' lag screws
2 lbs. 8 penny common nails
¼ lb. 6 penny common nails
¼ lb. 8 penny finishing nails

1 lb. 16 penny common nails
3 pair type A framing anchors
7 pair type C framing anchors

* also available in other widths

13

SITE SELECTION

Position a patio or porch where it complements the exterior appearance of your home, is convenient to reach from within, and meets local building codes. These dictate how close you can build to the property line, to a septic tank field, etc. While it's more convenient to build a patio adjacent to an existing door, directions on page 60 tell how to remove a window to install an outside door, or cut an opening through a wall.

Select a site that permits water to drain away, Illus. 2, rather than into area selected. A patio, built on high ground, should not be less than 3½" above grade at the lowest point.

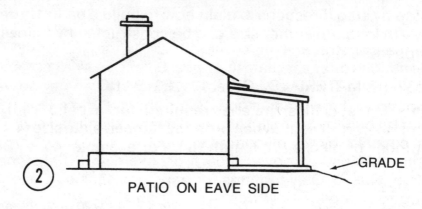

② PATIO ON EAVE SIDE

GRADE

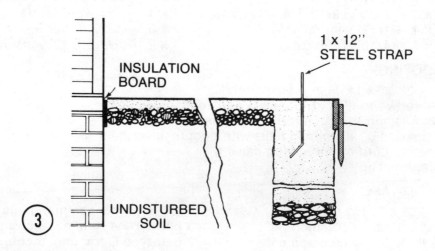

1 x 12"
STEEL STRAP

INSULATION
BOARD

③ UNDISTURBED
SOIL

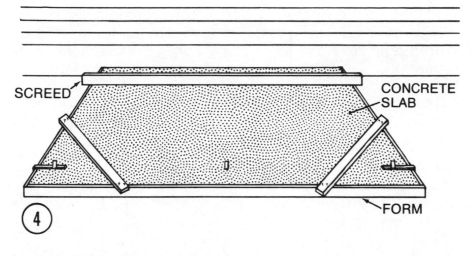

SCREED CONCRETE SLAB FORM

(4)

Since construction must meet many different conditions,* directions offer alternate methods. Select the one best suited to your site. If you have a level site adjacent to where you want a patio and the grade slopes away and not into site, a patio can be built by laying 3" of gravel over undisturbed soil. This is covered by 2" of concrete, Illus. 3. It can be finished smooth, Illus. 4, grooved, Illus. 5, or covered with flagstone or slate, Illus. 6. Only footings for patio posts, Illus. 7, need be dug to a depth below frost level.

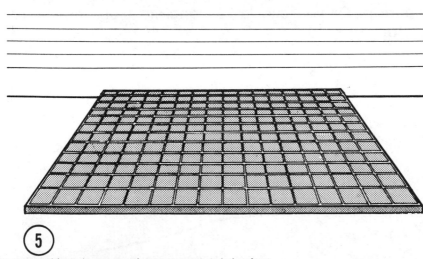

(5)

*In areas subjected to severe winters, excavate to below frost level. Fill with fieldstone, then gravel.

15

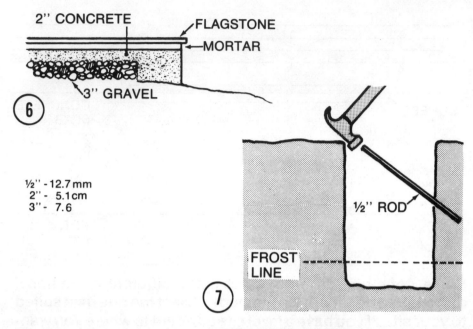

2" CONCRETE   FLAGSTONE
                MORTAR

3" GRAVEL

⑥

½" - 12.7 mm
2" - 5.1 cm
3" - 7.6

½" ROD

FROST
LINE

⑦

Where a site requires fill to raise above grade, or grade slopes sharply, Illus. 8, a perimeter foundation will be required on three sides. No foundation is required alongside the house. A perimeter foundation can be poured concrete or concrete block.

You will need to erect forms before pouring a concrete perimeter foundation, Illus. 9. Pour slab and foundation in one pouring. Or you can lay a concrete block perimeter foundation, Illus. 10.

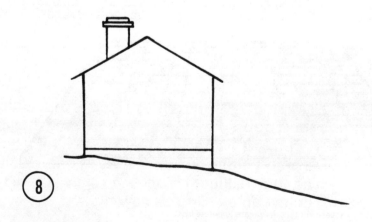

⑧

16

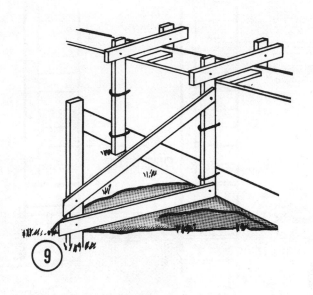

9

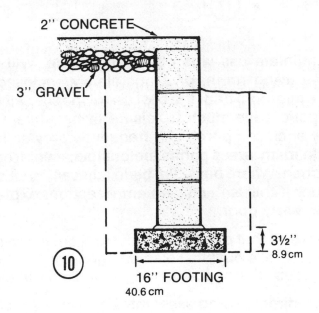

2" CONCRETE

3" GRAVEL

3½"
8.9 cm

10

16" FOOTING
40.6 cm

If site selected is on high ground with a steep slope, Illus. 8,
building forms for a poured concrete foundation, or laying
concrete block, permits filling area for slab. When com-
pacted, gravel laid to height required, a flagstone or slate
patio can finish as shown, Illus. 11; one step, Illus. 12; or two
steps, Illus. 13, below an existing or new door.

17

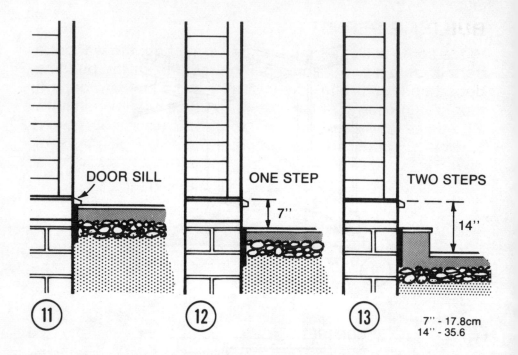

DOOR SILL

ONE STEP 7"

TWO STEPS 14"

⑪　　　⑫　　　⑬

7" - 17.8cm
14" - 35.6

Consider ultimate use when selecting a site. Will a patio alongside a living room, or a completely enclosed porch alongside a bedroom offer the best use of the site selected? A screened patio adds much to leisure living while a raised, completely enclosed porch can frequently provide an extra bedroom. In many areas patios are built adjacent to a dining area or kitchen. Where possible, build adjacent to an existing exterior door. If this isn't convenient, directions explain how to install an entry door.

Select a location that provides the desired quiet, privacy and convenience. Stake out site selected, then note how the sun may affect its use during the period you will most likely use it.

Step by step direction and assembly illustrations provide all the information needed to build a patio, porch or carport to size desired. Those who do little or none of the actual construction can still make substantial savings when they buy material and plan on being around when work is being done. Those who assist by doing what they are capable of doing soon discover it not only speeds production, but also insures getting better construction.

18

BUILDING PERMIT

While some codes permit construction of a patio without a permit, obtain one if same is required. Phone the building department and follow their advice. If the building department requires a plot plan, draw an outline as shown in Illus. 14. Add all the dimensions they specify. Since a patio, porch, carport or sundeck increases the value and appearance of your home, don't hesitate to build to a suitable size.

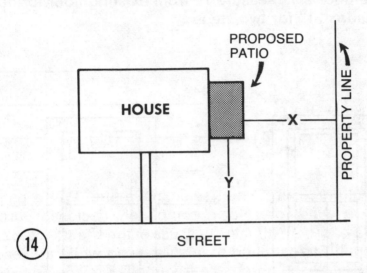

When submitting a plan for the proposed construction to the building inspector, he will want to know overall size of your property, location of existing buildings, distance from property lines, and exact location of the new construction. They will also want "estimated cost of construction." Use the cost of material provided by retailer. If they balk at the estimate, suggest they estimate manhours of labor required and rate of pay. Their estimate of overall cost can easily be questioned.

The Board of Health will want to know distance of proposed building from a septic tank and field. Water and gas lines passing under selected site normally present no problem. These can be channeled through an open end box before pouring footings, note page 27. A waste line to a sewer or septic tank does present a problem.

HOW TO LAY OUT GUIDE LINES

After selecting a site, decide height of finished patio floor below an existing door sill. Measure 7" down for one step, 14" for two steps. Draw a level line. This line indicates top of patio floor adjacent to house.

If there is no outside door, measure distance X, Illus. 15. Go outside and measure same distance X, Illus. 16. Add 2¼" for an outside door sill. Measure 7" from existing floor for one step, measure 14" for two steps.

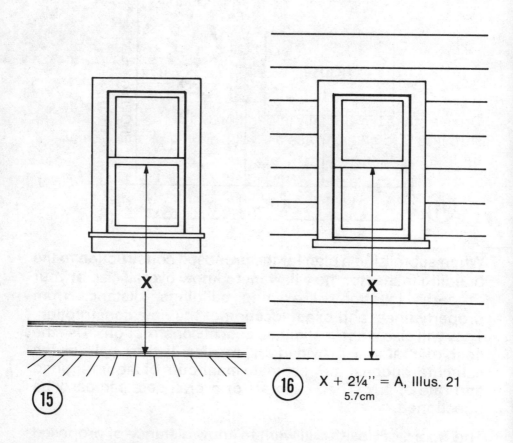

15

16 X + 2¼" = A, Illus. 21
5.7cm

To keep water from running into or against house, always slope a patio floor ⅛" to each foot of width. A 12' wide patio will slope a total of 1½" from level at house.

Temporarily drive two stakes against house, Illus. 17, 20' apart, or overall length of patio. Drive nails in stakes. Tie a line to nails to indicate exact length and height of patio floor against house.

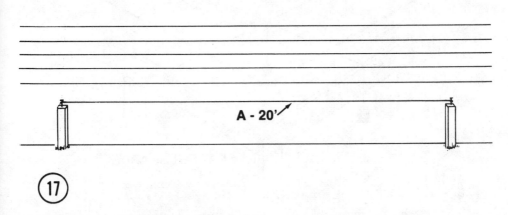

Drive a stake temporarily in position, 15' from house, Illus. 18. Run line B to stake. Place a line level on line and when level, tie line to stake.

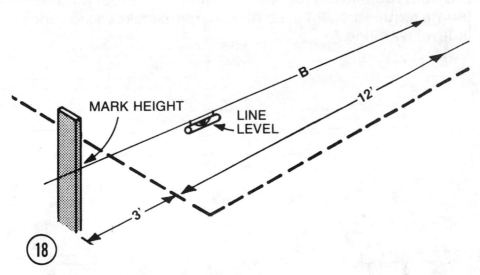

3' - 91.4cm
12' - 365.8
20' - 609.6

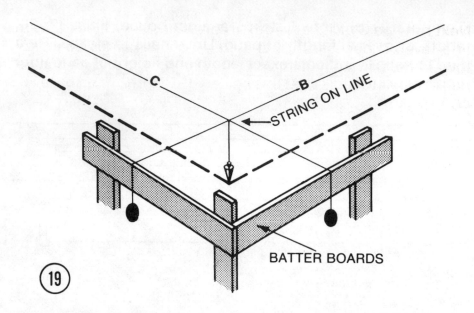

C

B
STRING ON LINE

BATTER BOARDS

⑲

Using 1 x 4's sharpened at one end for stakes, erect batter boards, Illus. 19, 3' from 12 x 20' area, Illus. 20. Tie a piece of string to line B to indicate 12' or width of patio. The extra 3' provides room to dig foundation trenches to exact width and length required. Nail 1 x 4 batter boards to stakes so top edge is level with line A.

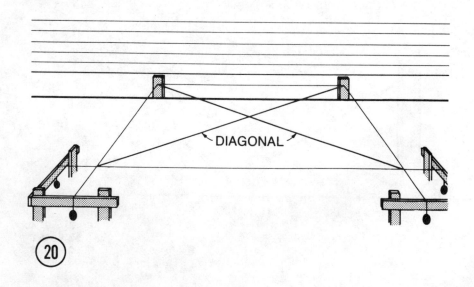

DIAGONAL

⑳

Next run line C at 12' or width of patio, Illus. 21. Check C with line level. If necessary, make a saw cut in batter board to lower line. Drive a nail into top of batter board and tie line to nail in order to raise it. At this point, line B and C must be level and square.

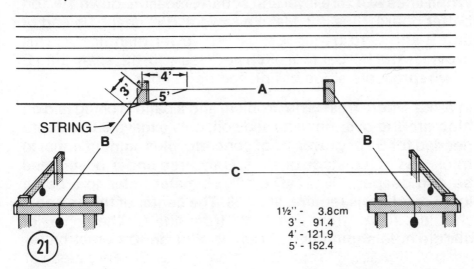

1½" - 3.8cm
3' - 91.4
4' - 121.9
5' - 152.4

To square lines, measure 4' on A, Illus. 21. Tie a piece of string or drive a nail temporarily into house to indicate 4' mark. Measure 3' on line B and tie a piece of string. Hook end of steel tape to 4' mark on A. Retie line B to batter board when 5' mark on tape crosses 3' mark on B.

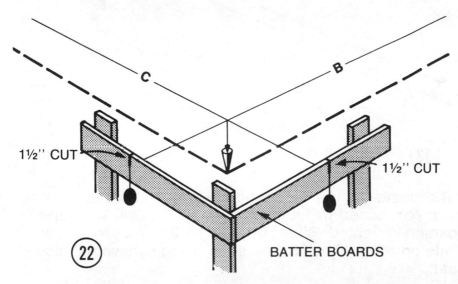

Do the same with other line B. To make certain lines are square, measure diagonals, Illus. 20. Lines are considered square when diagonals are equal length. When lines are square, double check to make certain they are level.

When lines ABC are level and square, measure down 1½" on batter board, Illus. 22. Make a sawcut 1½" deep. Tie end of line B and C to batter boards 1½" lower than line A. This provides the ⅛" per foot pitch necessary for 12' span. Line B now represents slope of finished patio floor.

In areas where frost is no problem and a patio is being laid on high ground over undisturbed soil, only excavate to a depth needed for 3" of gravel, 2" of concrete, plus amount equal to thickness of flagstone or slate. Only area under posts need be dug deeper, Illus. 7. Dig 12" diameter holes to a depth local conditions require, Illus. 23. The center of the end post should be 9¼" from line B, 6" from line C. The center of middle hole should be 10' from B, 6" from C.

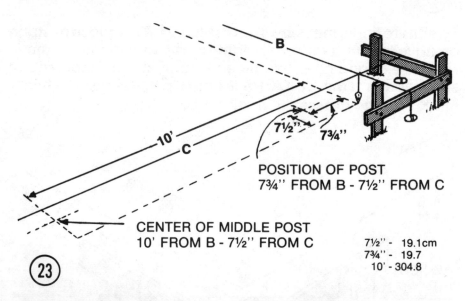

B

10'

C

7½"

7¾"

POSITION OF POST
7¾" FROM B - 7½" FROM C

CENTER OF MIDDLE POST
10' FROM B - 7½" FROM C

7½" - 19.1cm
7¾" - 19.7
10' - 304.8

(23)

Patio posts should be anchored to a 3/16 x 1 x 12" steel strap embedded in foundation, Illus. 24. Drill ¼" holes in position indicated. Fasten this to a 1 x 2 or 1 x 4 to hold strap while pouring, Illus. 25. The strap is lag screwed to side of post.

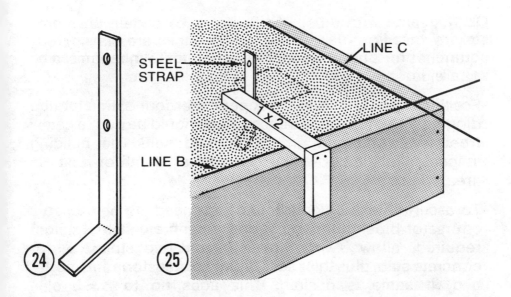

STEEL STRAP

LINE C

1 x 2

LINE B

24

25

In areas subjected to high winds, embed two foot lengths of ½" reinforcing rod crosswise, Illus. 26. Bend rod before pouring.

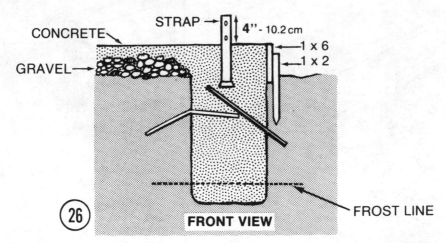

CONCRETE

GRAVEL

STRAP → 4" - 10.2 cm

1 x 6

1 x 2

26

FRONT VIEW

FROST LINE

Where site requires a poured concrete perimeter foundation, build forms, Illus. 9. Book #697 Forms, Footings, Foundation, Framing, Stair Building, provides complete details concerning erection of prefabricated as well as build-it-yourself forms.

A concrete block perimeter foundation, Illus. 10, is easier to build.

EXCAVATION

Trenches for a poured concrete perimeter foundation can be 12" wide.

Footings for a concrete block perimeter foundation require digging a two foot wide trench. Both should be dug to below frost level and laid on undisturbed soil. The building inspector or lumber dealer can advise "depth of frost" in area.

To ascertain exact depth foundation needs to be dug so a course of block permits pouring a concrete slab at height required, allow 3" for gravel or crushed stone, 2" for concrete slab, plus thickness of slate or flagstone and mortar bed, if same is desired. This adds up to 3 + 2 plus approximately 1" for mortar, 1 to 1½" for slate or flagstone, plus 3½" for footing form, Illus. 27.

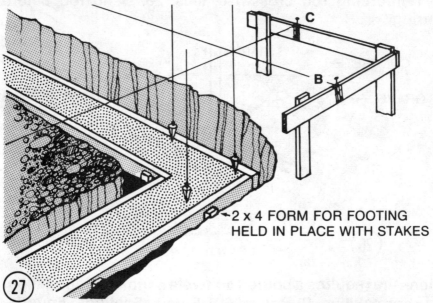

C

B

~2 x 4 FORM FOR FOOTING
HELD IN PLACE WITH STAKES

(27)

To lay 8x8x16" block, measure approximately 10½" down from line C and add 8" for every course of block required to reach frost level. Dig a two foot wide trench. This provides space to set up 2 x 4 footing forms 16" apart. 2 x 4's should be set up on undisturbed soil. Allow footings to set three days before laying block. See page 35.

PERIMETER FOUNDATION FOR SLAB ON GRADE

Those laying a slab on grade should set up guide lines, dig a 12" wide trench around perimeter, then dig post holes for footings to below frost level. Use 2 x 6, 2 x 8 or ½" plywood cut to width required for forms. These should be erected to height required by lines ABC, less thickness of flagstone or slate. This permits pouring a perimeter foundation and slab on grade in one pouring.

Hold forms in place by driving 1 x 2 or 1 x 4 stakes, Illus. 3. Top edge of form should slope to line B. Nail stakes to form. Nail 1 x 2 or 1 x 4 across corners to stiffen form, Illus. 28. If necessary, backfill outside of form to hold in place.

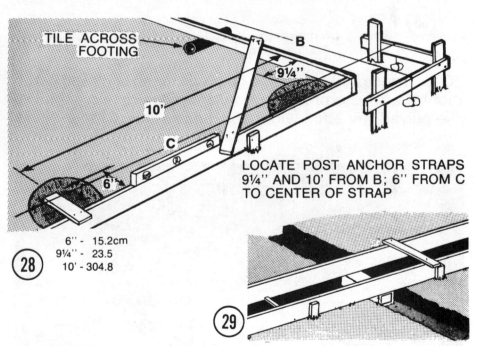

TILE ACROSS FOOTING

B

9¼"

10'

C

6"

LOCATE POST ANCHOR STRAPS 9¼" AND 10' FROM B; 6" FROM C TO CENTER OF STRAP

6" - 15.2cm
9¼" - 23.5
10' - 304.8

28

29

If you plan on running underground electric service, telephone, hi fi or water line to patio, these should be laid before spreading gravel. Run lines through a 4 or 6" diameter tile below form, Illus. 28. Or make an open end box using four 1 x 6 x 16", Illus. 29. Knock this out after concrete sets. If you use tile, it remains in place. This sleeve permits running service lines under perimeter of foundation.

Before pouring slab, nail a strip of ½ x 4 or 6'' wide asphalt impregnated insulation board the full length of patio, Illus. 3, 30. Position top edge ½'' below line A. This provides an expansion joint for slab.

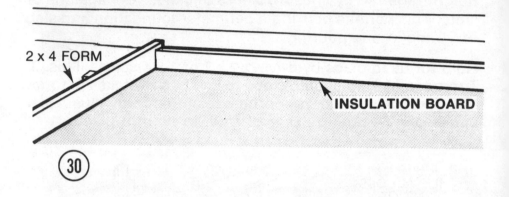

2 x 4 FORM

INSULATION BOARD

30

NOTE: Those building a slab on grade for an enclosed porch should lay a waterproof polyethylene membrane over gravel. Use polyethylene full width and length, Illus. 31.

GRAVEL　WATERPROOF MEMBRANE　6 x 6 WIRE

31

Lay 6 x 6 steel reinforcing wire, Illus. 32, over gravel. Position wire within 1'' from edge. Raise wire 1'' (or half the thickness of slab) above gravel. Use globs of concrete every 3' to raise wire.

CONCRETE

(32)

Next position a 2 x 4 approximately 18 to 24'' away from house, Illus. 33. Keep top face level with outside form. Support 2 x 4 with globs of concrete. The 2 x 4 provides a support when screeding concrete, Illus. 34.

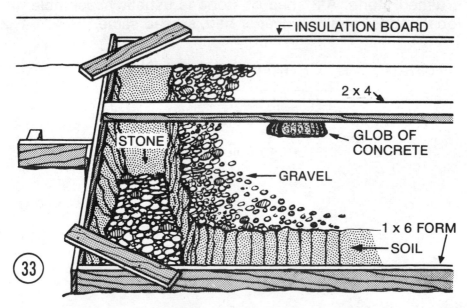

INSULATION BOARD

2 x 4

GLOB OF CONCRETE

STONE

GRAVEL

1 x 6 FORM

SOIL

(33)

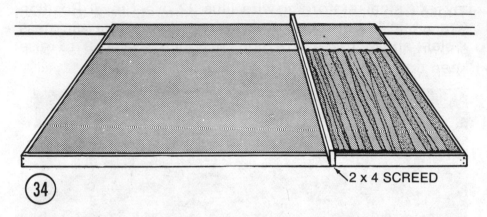

(34)

2 x 4 SCREED

Those who plan on mixing concrete should only buy as many bags of cement as they can use during the period they plan on working. Don't store cement from week to week. Buy sand in five to seven yard quantities to obtain the best price. If you buy readymix, excavate area to depth required. Tell dealer overall size of the area and thickness you want to spread gravel, also thickness of slab.

He will estimate the exact amount of run of bank gravel or crushed stone and concrete required. Run of bank gravel can frequently be purchased at considerably less cost than ¾" crushed stone. A 3" bed of stone is usually acceptable. If local codes require a deeper bed, spread same.

1" - 2.54cm

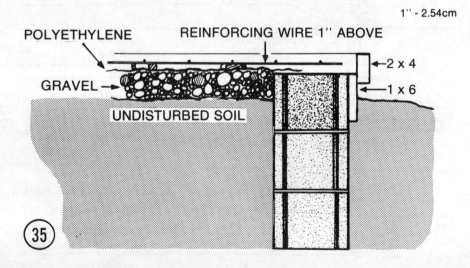

POLYETHYLENE   REINFORCING WIRE 1" ABOVE

2 x 4

GRAVEL

1 x 6

UNDISTURBED SOIL

(35)

Those who want slate, flagstone or concrete floor to project over edge of foundation should nail a 1 x 6 to 2 x 4 in position shown, Illus. 35. Paint inside face with old crankcase oil to keep concrete from sticking.

Position form in place by nailing to stakes, Illus. 36. Top edge of form should pitch to line BC. Check corners to make certain they are square and at proper height. Hold corners square by nailing 1 x 2 diagonally across, Illus. 37.

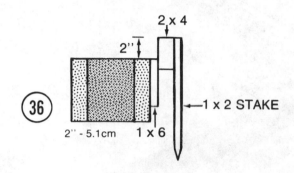

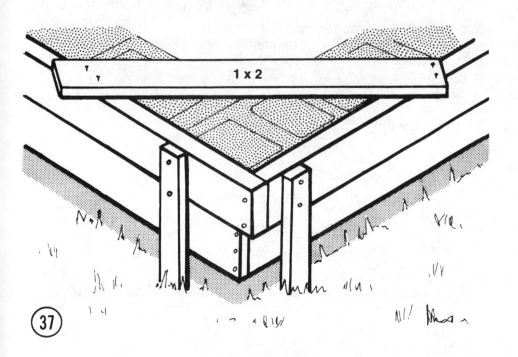

NOTE: Those laying a slab on grade or a concrete block perimeter foundation must embed anchor straps in exact position each post requires. Illus. 38 indicates position of posts when ¾'' lipped edge, Illus. 36, is planned.

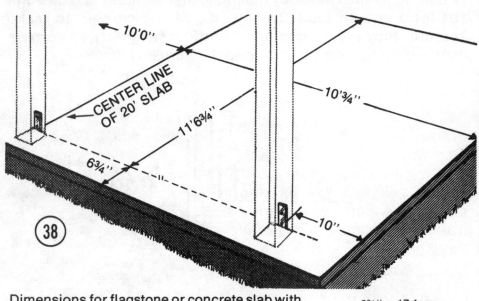

10'0''

CENTER LINE OF 20' SLAB

10'¾''

11'6¾''

6¾''

10''

(38)

Dimensions for flagstone or concrete slab with ¾'' lipped edge, Illus. 36, are approximate.

6¾'' - 17.1cm
10'' - 25.4
10' - 304.8
10'¾'' - 306.7
11'6¾'' - 352.4
20' - 609.6

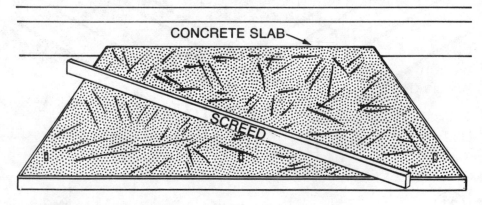

CONCRETE SLAB

SCREED

(39)

Spread and work concrete into all pockets and against form. Use care not to pierce polyethylene moisture barrier. Pour concrete in one day. Don't do part one day and balance later.

Use a straight 2 x 4 as a screed, Illus.34. Work it back and forth saw fashion to level concrete. Fill in area between 2 x 4 form and expansion joint. After screeding surface, place plank on wet concrete and remove 2 x 4 form. Fill void with concrete.

If you plan on laying flagstone or slate, allow the concrete to set slightly, then score it, Illus. 39.

Allow concrete to set up at least three days before applying flagstone or slate. If you tell the dealer the exact overall size of the patio, he will lay out all stone and provide a diagram showing where each is to be laid. He will also drill holes to accommodate anchor straps for posts if you provide accurate dimensions. Encourage the retailer to take dimensions if he can conveniently do so. Be sure to allow for overhang on three sides and for mortar joints if you lay out flagstone.

Before spreading mortar, make a dry run. Place all pieces in position to check amount of spacing each stone requires. The dry run requires handling a lot of stone, but it does help produce a professional job. After positioning, check with a straight 2 x 4 and a level to make certain patio pitches to outside. If it needs more pitch, lay a thicker bed of mortar. Start laying flagstone or slate along house. Always place stones according to the numbered layout dealer furnishes.

Lay flagstone or slate in a mortar bed consisting of one part cement to two parts finely screened sand. A 1'' thick mortar bed is usually sufficient.

Allow flagstone to set at least two days before grouting joints. Use one part cement to two parts finely screened sand for grout or buy a prepared grout. With trowel, work grout down between stones and scrape off flush with surface. Clean and wash surplus grout off face of stone as quickly as possible. Use a jointer, Illus. 40, to finish grouted joints. Allow deck to set at least three days before walking on it.

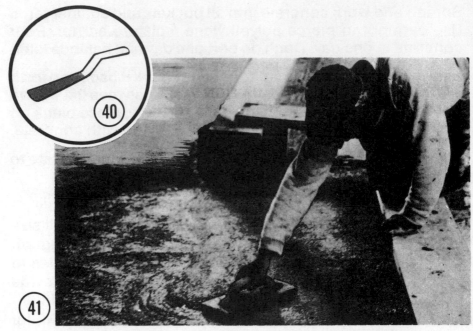

FLOAT METHOD OF FINISHING CONCRETE

If you prefer a finished concrete slab, no flagstone or slate, use a wood or steel float to finish surface. Work off a plank, Illus. 41. The wood float gives a slightly rougher finish. Keep dipping float in a pail of water to obtain a smooth finish. Don't over trowel. Too much floating tends to create a finish that makes dust. Those wishing to groove surface should use a groover and a 2 x 4 as a straight edge, Illus. 42.

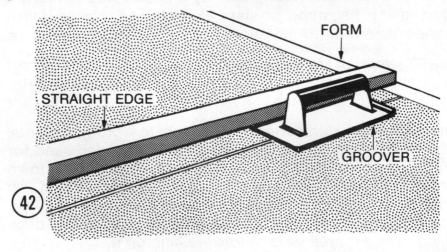

FORM

STRAIGHT EDGE

GROOVER

Many retailers rent machines that permit floating concrete to a marble like finish. Follow manufacturer's directions when using same. If you want to groove the concrete slab, you can buy, borrow or rent a groover from your concrete dealer. Use this with a straight 2 x 4. Grooving must be done just as concrete begins to set. Test a little concrete and note best time.

FOOTINGS FOR A CONCRETE BLOCK PERIMETER FOUNDATION

Footings for concrete block perimeter foundation should be laid below frost level on undisturbed soil, Illus. 10. No footings or block are required alongside house. 2 x 4's are usually sufficient for a footing form. Space the 2 x 4 forms 16" apart for 8 x 8 x 16" blocks. Drop a plumb line down from lines B and C and space form so outside face of block is 4" in from edge of footing, Illus. 27. The outside face and end of corner block will be plumb with line BC, Illus. 43.

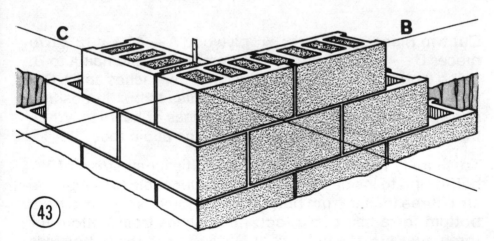

Use a straight 2 x 4 and a level to check form. Also check height to guide line C to make certain space allows for slab, mortar, flagstone and gravel, and balance is divisible by 8. You can throw any fieldstone available into the footing form, then cover with concrete consisting of one part cement, three parts sand to five parts ¾" gravel. Remove 2 x 4 forms three days after footings set up.

Those mixing concrete for footings or slab should use a bottomless measuring box, Illus. 44.

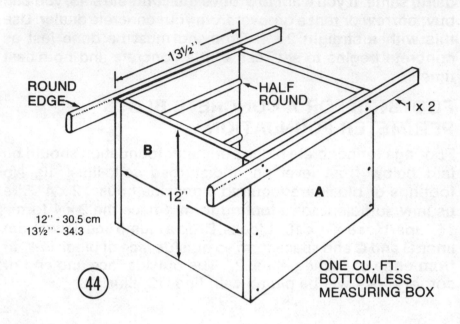

ROUND EDGE

HALF ROUND

1 x 2

B

A

13½"

12"

12" - 30.5 cm
13½" - 34.3

44

ONE CU. FT.
BOTTOMLESS
MEASURING BOX

Cut two pieces of ½, ⅝ or ¾" plywood A — 13½ x 12"; two pieces B — 12 x 12". Apply waterproof glue and nail A to B, using 8 penny common nails spaced three inches apart. Cut two 1 x 2 x 24" for handles. Nail handles to box in position shown. Use a file or rasp to round edges of handles. When filled level with top, measure holds one cubic foot.

To simplify measuring smaller quantities, nail strips of ⅜" half-round to inside of box. For a quarter cubic foot, nail one strip three inches from bottom; nail another six inches from bottom for a half cubic foot; nine inches from bottom for three quarters of a cubic foot. Always place the bottomless measure in mortar tub. When you fill the amount required, remove measure.

A bag of Portland cement weighs 94 lbs.* It is equal to one cubic foot. One bag of cement, 2¼ cubic feet of sand, plus 3 cubic feet of gravel and between 4 to 5½ gallons of water make approximately 4½ cubic feet of concrete.

*87.5 lbs. in Canada

Before laying block, check guide lines to make certain they are square, level and taut. Check diagonals. Setting blocks takes some skill, common sense and practice. You gain valuable knowledge working alongside an experienced mason. Most masons use a mortar consisting of one bag of Portland cement, a third to half bag of mason's lime, 20 to 24 shovels of sand. This usually takes 6 to 6½ gallons of water. A skilled mason uses mortar on the firm side, not too wet, not too dry. Watch one work and note the consistency he uses.

Spread 1'' of mortar over corner area and to about 2' from corner. Drop a plumb bob down from guide line to mark mortar at corner and again about two feet from corner. With straight edge and trowel, draw a line in mortar to indicate exact corner. Set corner block level and plumb with guide line. Set another block in mortar at other end of footing, Illus. 45. Tap each block into place and check with level.

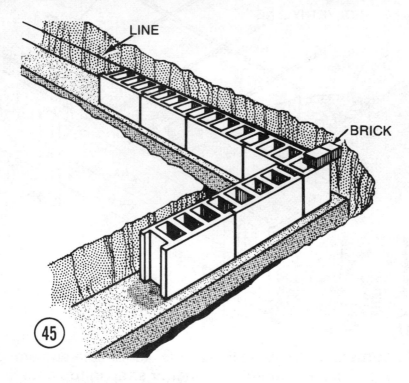

LINE

BRICK

45

Stretch a line along outside edge of first course. Hold line taut by wrapping ends around brick placed temporarily on top of blocks. Check line with level. Butter up end of each block, Illus. 46, before placing in position. Drop plumb bob down from guide line as you work to make certain blocks are laid to line. Stagger joints on each course.

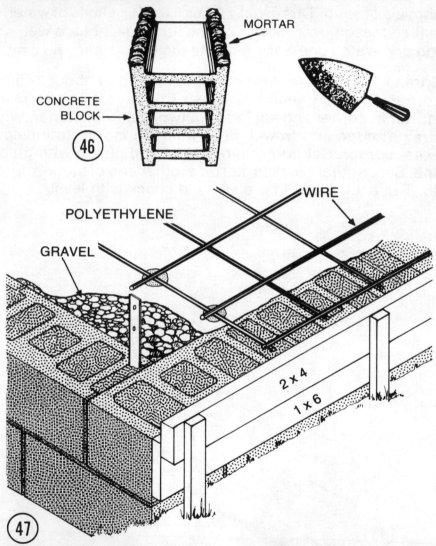

MORTAR

CONCRETE BLOCK →

46

WIRE

POLYETHYLENE

GRAVEL

2 x 4

1 x 6

47

Build corners up to guide lines, Illus. 43. Locate and embed ⅛ x 1 x 12″ steel or aluminum anchor strap in top course in position posts require. Allow strap to project amount required for slab and flagstone. Blocks on top course are laid level and to height below line C that allows for slab, mortar and flagstone. The crushed stone or gravel is laid level with top of block, Illus. 47.

Spread polyethylene*and/or reinforcing wire as previously described on page 28.

For a 2" concrete slab, measure down 2" from top edge of 2 x 4 and snap a line. Nail 1 x 6 along line, Illus. 36. Nail assembled 1 x 6 and 2 x 4 to stakes so top of 2 x 4 slopes to pitch and is 2 to 3" or amount below B required for flagstone and mortar. Allow slab to begin to set, then score it as previously described. Allow slab to cure three days, then apply mortar bed, slate or flagstone.

Spread mortar mix consisting of one part cement to two parts finely screened sand alongside house. Position flagstone following numbered diagram retailer provides. Use mortar mix retailer suggests for grouting flagstone. Use a jointer tool, Illus. 40, to finish joints. Apply grout or calking to joint between house and flagstone. Allow grout to set at least three days before starting framing.

Those who prefer laying 6 x 6" paver tile should follow directions offered in Book #606 How to Lay Ceramic Tile.

HOW TO ADD COLOR TO CONCRETE PATIO

A concrete patio deck can be colored with masonry powders. Your lumber yard can supply a wide selection of colors.

The best time to add color is when you are laying concrete. First prepare a dry mix of color powder with white Portland cement. Mix in proportion to manufacturer's recommendations. Do not add water; keep dry.

Lay concrete slab to within ½ to 1" from top of form. Add dry sand to your color and add to concrete in proportion recommended. Mix well. Finish laying concrete. For pastel shades, use less color in proportion to a bag of cement. Always apply color following manufacturer's recommendations.

*For an enclosed area.

FRAMING A PATIO

Since lumber varies in width and thickness, always check dimension so you can cut inner framing members to size required. Most framing lumber now runs to following sizes:
1 x 2 — ¾ x 1½'', 1 x 4 — ¾ x 3½'', 1 x 10 — ¾ x 9¼'',
2 x 4 — 1½ x 3½'', 2 x 6 — 1½ x 5½'', 4 x 4 — 3½ x 3½''.

After cutting to length and angle required, paint with wood preservative. When thoroughly dry, apply at least one coat of exterior paint.

Use dimension lumber local codes specify. Many codes permit using 2 x 6 for patio rafters on spans up to 12', 2 x 8 on spans up to 16'.

Illus. 48 shows framing required for a 12' wide patio. A full size angle pattern, Illus. 49, simplifies cutting rafter. Use as is or adjust angle if you wish more pitch.

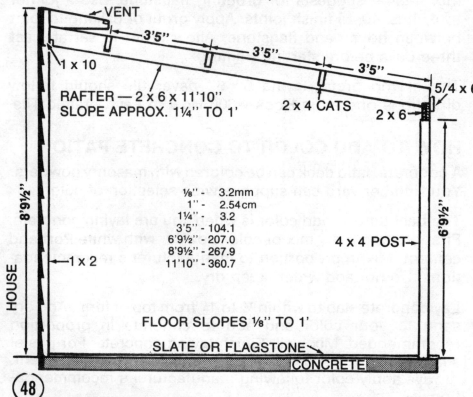

VENT

3'5''

3'5''

3'5''

1 x 10

5/4 x 6

RAFTER — 2 x 6 x 11'10''
SLOPE APPROX. 1¼'' TO 1'

2 x 4 CATS

2 x 6

8'9½''

⅛'' - 3.2mm
1'' - 2.54cm
1¼'' - 3.2
3'5'' - 104.1
6'9½'' - 207.0
8'9½'' - 267.9
11'10'' - 360.7

6'9½''

4 x 4 POST

HOUSE

1 x 2

FLOOR SLOPES ⅛'' TO 1'

SLATE OR FLAGSTONE

CONCRETE

48

40

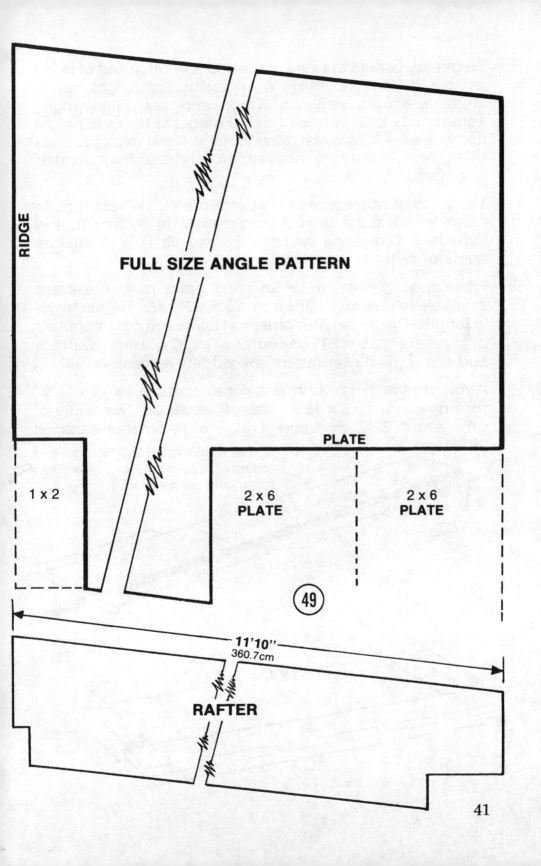

RIDGE

FULL SIZE ANGLE PATTERN

PLATE

1 x 2

2 x 6 PLATE

2 x 6 PLATE

(49)

11'10"
360.7cm

RAFTER

41

To get dry behind the ears, trace and saw ridge end of rafter pattern on a 1 x 6. Place it in position at height noted. Measure length required. Trace and saw plate angle. Temporarily tack a piece of 1 x 10 (ridge) to house at height noted, Illus. 48. Tack test rafter to ridge. If test rafter provides pitch and headroom needed, cut rafters from lumber specified.

The pitch of rafter offered is approximately 1¼" per foot. In areas where there is no snow, a pitch of ¾" per foot is sufficient. Directions on page 56 explain how to change angle of rafter to meet local codes.

Fiber glass panels make an ideal patio roof. These are available in varying widths from 25½, 33½ and 40", up to 16' in length. The 25" width overlaps at joints and can be applied over rafters spaced 24" on centers. The 33½" width overlaps and are applied over rafters spaced 32" on centers.

If you use the 33½" width, draw lines across a 1 x 10 x 18'9" for ridge, and 2 x 6 x 18'9" plate, Illus. 50, 51. The center of first rafter is 32½" from end of ridge, while others are spaced 32" apart.

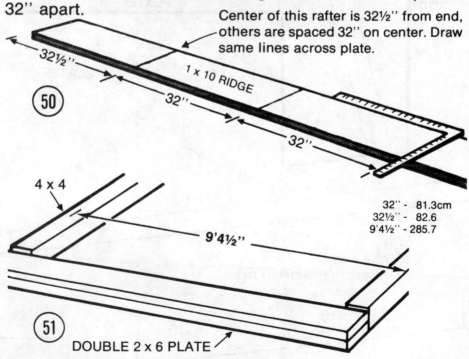

Center of this rafter is 32½" from end, others are spaced 32" on center. Draw same lines across plate.

32½"

1 x 10 RIDGE

(50)

32"

32"

4 x 4

9'4½"

32" - 81.3cm
32½" - 82.6
9'4½" - 285.7

(51)

DOUBLE 2 x 6 PLATE

Use a square to locate and draw lines. Always space rafters to meet local snow loads. Follow manufacturer's specifications for width of panel selected.

Cut three 4 x 4 posts 6'9½''. These can be cut slightly shorter if a second floor window necessitates lowering ridge nailed to house. Under no circumstances cut post less than 6'6''.

Nail a 1 x 2 flush with bottom edge of 1 x 10 ridge, Illus. 52.

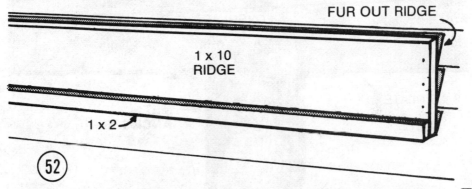

FUR OUT RIDGE

1 x 10 RIDGE

1 x 2

(52)

Nail strips of clapboard or wood shingle to fur out 1 x 10 ridge. This permits nailing ridge plumb. If necessary, use two lengths of 1 x 10 for the 18'9'' ridge.

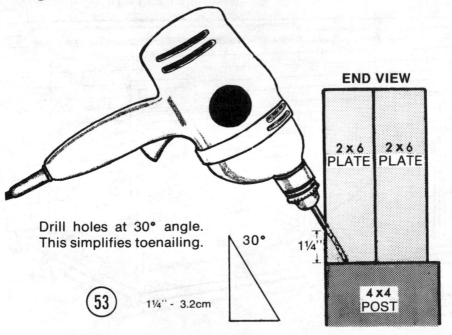

END VIEW

2 x 6 PLATE   2 x 6 PLATE

Drill holes at 30° angle. This simplifies toenailing.

30°

1¼''

4 x 4 POST

(53)   1¼'' - 3.2cm

Cut two 2 x 6 x 20' to 18'9'', or use two 2 x 6 x 12' and two 2 x 6 x 8' for plate, Illus. 51. Stagger joints. Spike together with 16 penny common nails. Cut to length. Toenail plate to top of post, Illus. 53, flush with outside face, using 8 penny common nails. Drill holes to accurately drive nails, or use metal fasteners, Illus. 54, available at lumber dealers. These increase strength of joint. Center middle post.

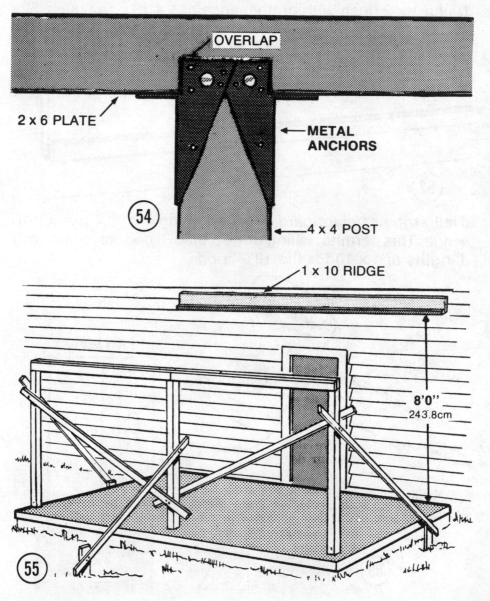

OVERLAP

2 x 6 PLATE

METAL ANCHORS

54

4 x 4 POST

1 x 10 RIDGE

8'0''
243.8cm

55

Raise and brace plate in plumb position, Illus. 55. Check each post with level in two directions. Hold with temporary bracing. Shim post with slate if necessary. Fasten anchor strap to posts with ¼ x 2" lag screws. Flush concrete under post if required.

Illus. 48, 55 indicate suggested height for 1 x 10 ridge. Check ridge with level and spike in place with 16 penny nails driven into studs.

When attaching a ridge board to a brick, concrete block or other masonry wall, use expansion shields 24" on centers, Illus. 56. Drill ¼" holes through ridge. Locate and drill holes in masonry using a carbide tipped bit. Use size required for expansion shields purchased.

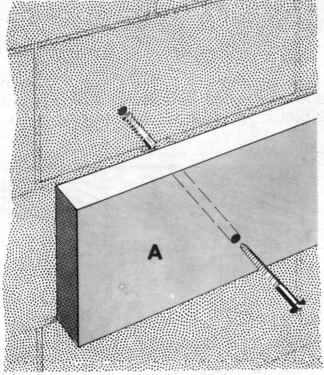

56

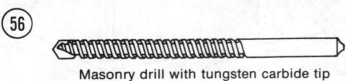

Masonry drill with tungsten carbide tip

Before cutting rafters, sight down each and keep the crown edge up, Illus. 57.

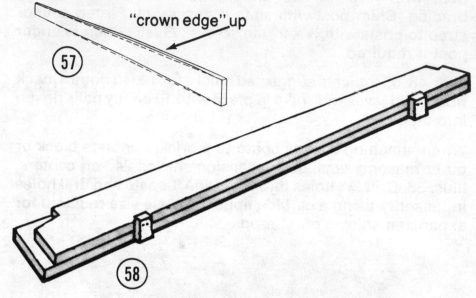

"crown edge" up

57

58

Cut one rafter to angle of pattern, Illus. 49. Again, test in position and adjust angle if necessary. If OK, use as a pattern. Nail 1 x 2 blocks, Illus. 58. Trace and cut rafters needed.

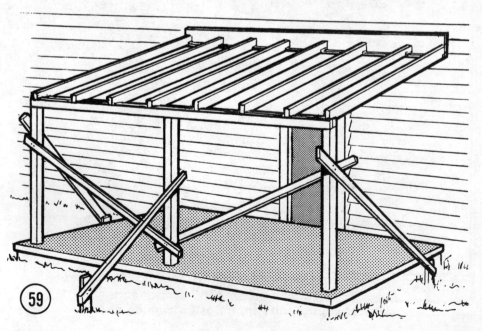

59

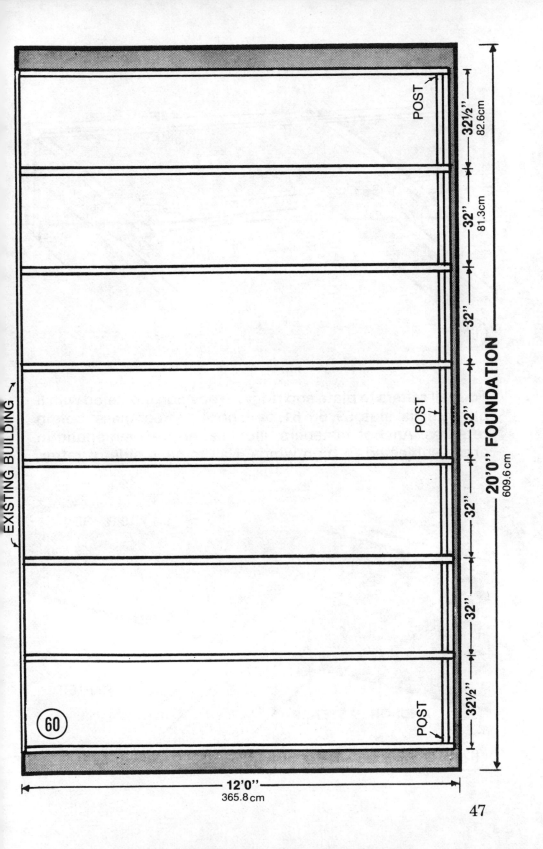

EXISTING BUILDING

POST

POST

POST

60

32½" 82.6cm

32" 81.3cm

32"

32"

32"

32"

32½"

20'0" FOUNDATION
609.6 cm

12'0"
365.8 cm

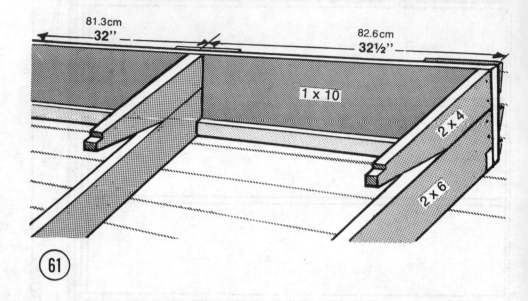

81.3cm
32"

82.6cm
32½"

1 x 10

2 x 4

2 x 6

61

Toenail rafters to plate and ridge, in position indicated with 8 penny nails, Illus. 59, 60, 61, or in position fiber glass roofing requires. Anchor fasteners, Illus. 62, are recommended in areas subjected to high winds. Nail to each side of rafter.

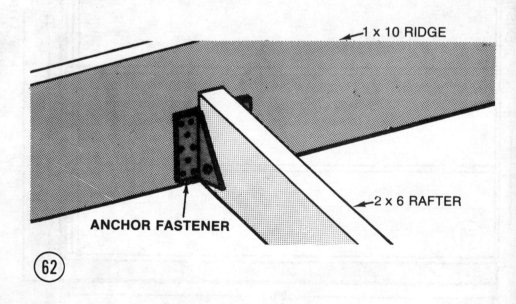

1 x 10 RIDGE

2 x 6 RAFTER

ANCHOR FASTENER

62

VENT RAFTERS

The engineered air vent in the roof of the Easi-Bild patio, Illus. 48, 63, stimulates a free flow of air. This not only insures a cooler patio, but also helps keep adjacent rooms cooler.

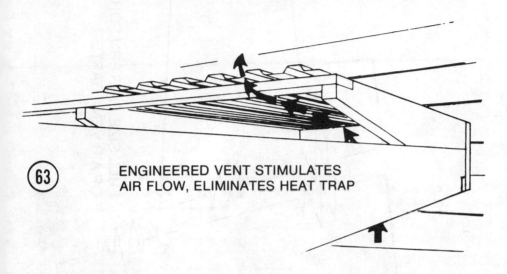

(63) ENGINEERED VENT STIMULATES AIR FLOW, ELIMINATES HEAT TRAP

Cut 2 x 4 vent rafters, Illus. 61, 63, to length and angle shown, Illus. 64, 65, or to angle of rafter if same has been revised. Toenail air vent rafter in position flush with each rafter, Illus. 48, 61.

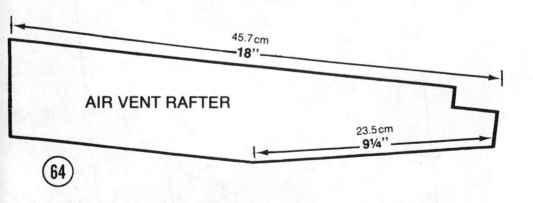

45.7cm
18"

AIR VENT RAFTER

23.5cm
9¼"

(64)

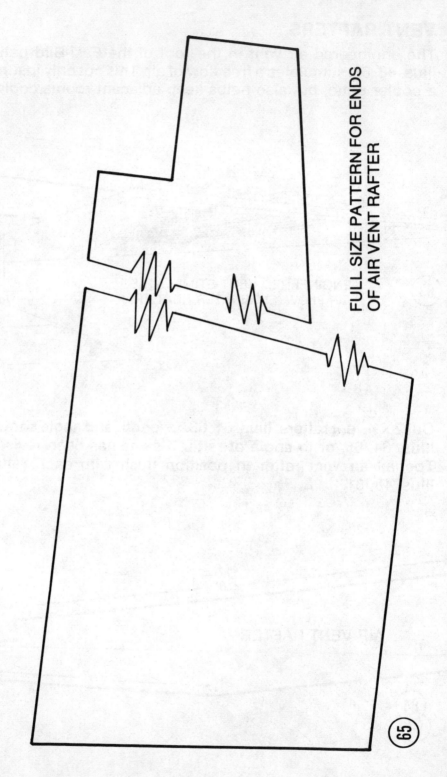

FULL SIZE PATTERN FOR ENDS
OF AIR VENT RAFTER

65

Cut 2 x 4 cats to length required. Nail in position, Illus. 48, 66, flush with top edge of rafter.

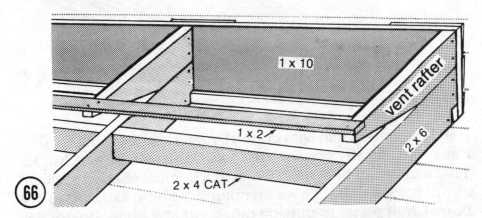

Cut 1 x 2 x 18'9''. If two lengths are needed, butt ends over center of a rafter. Nail in position to vent rafters using 6 penny nails, Illus. 66.

All framing should now be painted. Apply wood preservative following manufacturer's directions, then apply at least two coats of exterior paint. Allow to dry thoroughly before applying roofing panels.

Cut 33½'' width by 14' panels to length required to butt against bottom of vent rafter and project 1½'' beyond edge of plate, Illus. 67.

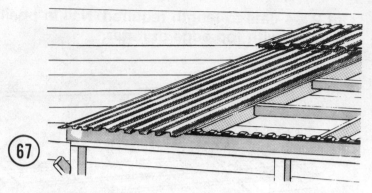

(67)

Nail first panel flush with edge of outside rafter, Illus. 68. Drill nail holes slightly smaller than nail. Use a twin thread, No. 10, 1¾" aluminum nail, Illus. 69, with a conical shaped resilient neoprene washer. The washer plugs the hole like a bung in a barrel. Nail panel to outside rafter, cat and plate. Do not nail along inside rafter.

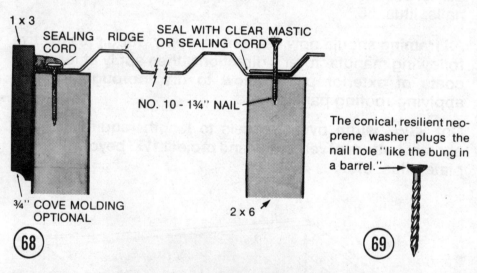

1 x 3

SEALING CORD   RIDGE   SEAL WITH CLEAR MASTIC OR SEALING CORD

NO. 10 - 1¾" NAIL

The conical, resilient neoprene washer plugs the nail hole "like the bung in a barrel."

¾" COVE MOLDING OPTIONAL

2 x 6

(68)   (69)

Using cutoff from panel, measure and cut 19" or length needed to project 1" over end of vent rafter. Drill and nail outside edge to vent rafter with three nails.

Nail flashing fiber glass manufacturer provides. Flashing can be applied in three different ways. You can first apply calking fiber glass manufacturer specifies, then face nail flashing in position, Illus. 70.

52

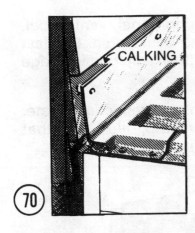

CALKING

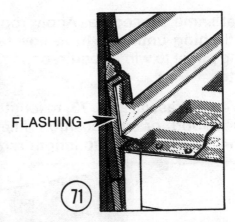

FLASHING→

70

71

COUNTER FLASHING

72

The question of when to apply flashing depends on length available. If matching flashing is available in lengths wider than panels, apply it following panel manufacturer's directions.

The second approach is to drive siding nails clear through siding. Use a nailset. Slide flashing up under a course of siding, Illus. 71. Nail through siding along top edge of flashing. Countersink heads. Fill holes with putty.

A third method is to nail flashing to siding, Illus. 72, then slide counter flashing (use a strip of aluminum or copper) under siding.

Apply a strand of sealing cord on top of first panel before applying second roofing panel, Illus. 68. Overlap panel as shown. Drill holes through both panels and nail. Use sealing cord or mastic fiber glass manufacturer specifies.

Repeat same procedure. Apply roofing panel, vent panel, then flashing until you have covered entire area. Cut last roofing panel to width required to fit flush with outside edge of rafter.

Cut 5/4 x 6" fascia, Illus. 73, to length required to face plate. Cut redwood or composition filler strip, Illus. 74, that matches roofing panel to length required.

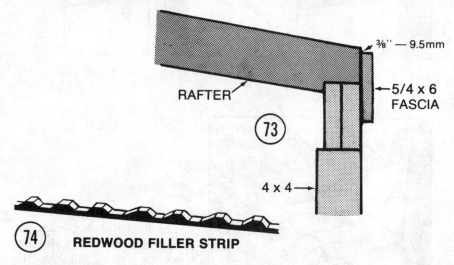

RAFTER

⅜" — 9.5mm

←5/4 x 6 FASCIA

73

4 x 4→

74 **REDWOOD FILLER STRIP**

Position filler strip on top of fascia, Illus. 75, so it matches roofing panel. Nail filler strip to fascia. Apply adhesive to filler strip if fiber glass manufacturer recommends same. Nail fascia to plate so filler strip butts snugly against panel. Drill holes and nail panel through filler strip into edge of fascia.

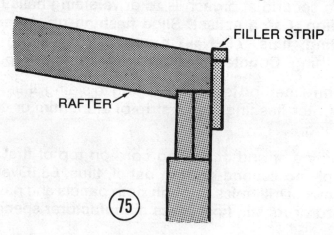

FILLER STRIP

RAFTER

75

Saw end of a 1 x 3 to shape shown, Illus. 76. Cut to length of rafter, Illus. 77, and nail in position. Keep top edge of 1 x 3 level with ridge of panel, Illus. 68.

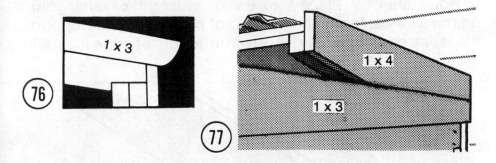

Cut 1 x 4 vent fascia to shape shown, Illus. 77. Nail in position above 1 x 3. Apply non-drying calking compound to joint between 1 x 3 and 1 x 4 and panel, Illus. 68, or apply sealing cord. This helps seal out water, dust and insects. Remove all bracing. Fill holes with wood filler and apply paint.

While this procedure lessens the need to work on top of fiber glass panels, if you do go topside, use non-skid rubber sole sneakers. Carefully position 2 x 8 planks across rafters. If pitch of roof creates a problem, tie ropes to 2 x 8 planks. Throw ropes over roof and tie to a 2 x 4 across inside of a window, Illus. 78.

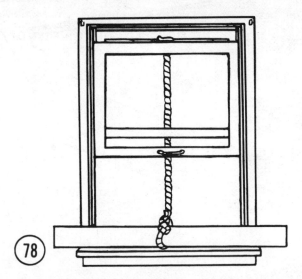

HOW TO CHANGE ANGLE OF RAFTER

The rafter pattern, Illus. 49, meets most needs. If you need to change pitch of rafter, follow this procedure. Don't nail 1 x 2 to ridge, Illus. 52. Place a 2 x 6 x 12, or length of rafter your patio requires, in position on top of plate, Illus. 79. Support ridge end on an 8 penny nail driven in bottom of ridge, Illus. 80.

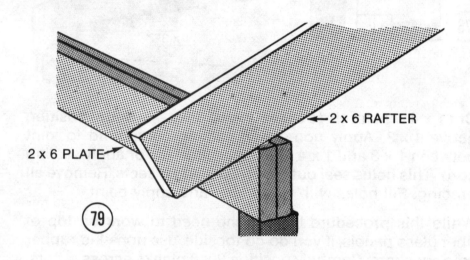

2 x 6 RAFTER

2 x 6 PLATE

(79)

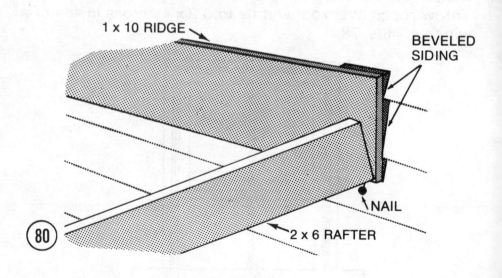

1 x 10 RIDGE

BEVELED SIDING

(80)

NAIL

2 x 6 RAFTER

Drive a nail 2'' below top edge of plate, Illus. 81. Place rafter on nail, Illus. 82.

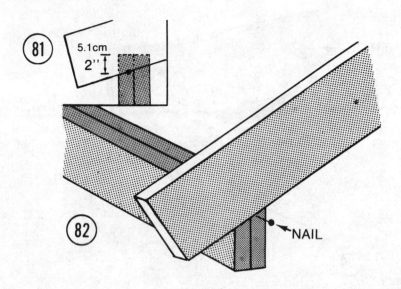

Place level in plumb position and draw line on rafter, Illus. 83. Remove and saw rafter to this line.

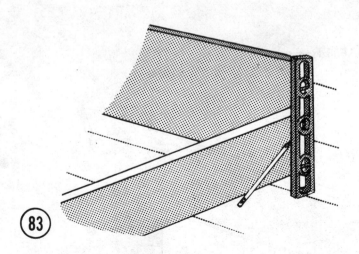

Nail 1 x 2 to ridge, Illus. 52. Notch ridge end of rafter to receive 1 x 2, Illus. 84.

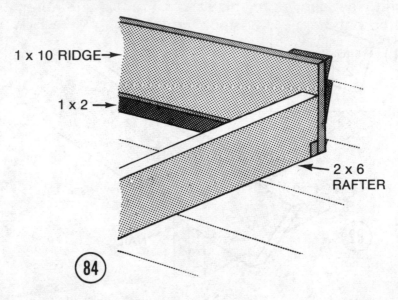

1 x 10 RIDGE→

1 x 2 →

← 2 x 6 RAFTER

84

Place rafter in position with ridge end on 1 x 2, plate end on nail. Mark outline of plate, Illus. 85. Remove and saw to shape required. When rafter checks out OK, use it as a pattern, Illus. 58, to cut others.

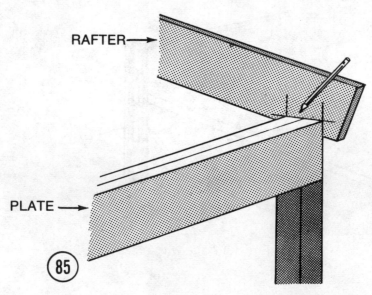

RAFTER→

PLATE →

85

OVERHANGING EAVE

If your house has an overhanging eave, Illus. 86, or a projecting second story, no vent rafters are required. A ventilated patio can be positioned as shown.

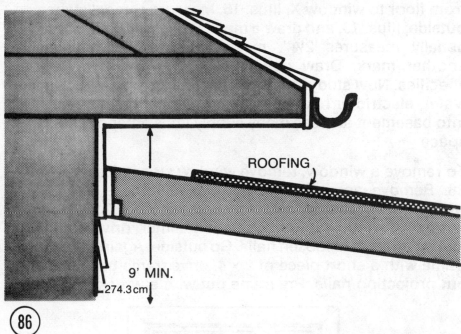

ROOFING

9' MIN.
274.3 cm

(86)

If space below projecting eave doesn't provide height required, fasten rafters in position to a ¾" exterior plywood ridge, Illus. 87. Cut ridge to full width pitch on roof requires. In this installation, apply counter flashing as shown in Illus. 72.

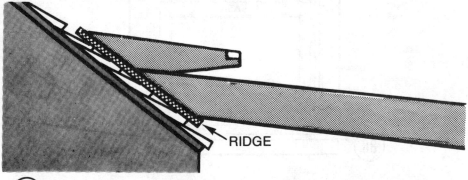

RIDGE

(87)   Fur out ridge with pieces of shingle.

HOW TO INSTALL AN OUTSIDE DOOR

When no outside door is convenient to site selected, and an existing window is located where a door is preferred, or a door needs to be cut through a blank wall, measure distance from floor to window X, Illus. 15. Measure same distance on outside, Illus. 16, and draw a mark. Since an outside door sill usually measures 2¼", measure down 2¼" and make another mark. Draw outline of opening to size retailer specifies. Now study location selected. Do any service lines, water, electric or heating lines cross location selected? Go into basement and see if any supply lines enter or cross this space.

To remove a window, remove window stops, casing B, Illus. 88. Remove apron D. Knock up and remove sill C. Still working from inside, place a short block of 2 x 4 against bottom of window frame. Using a hammer, drive frame out just far enough to loosen nails. Go outside. Again, protecting frame with a short piece of 2 x 4, drive frame back and pull out projecting nails. Pry frame out with a wrecking bar.

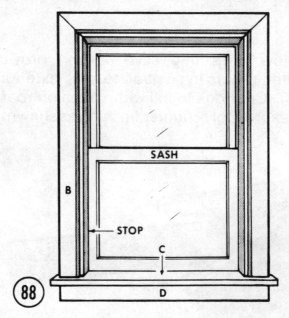

SASH

B

STOP

C

88

D

After making double certain no electrical, water or heating lines cross area selected, saw exterior siding, subsheathing, inside plaster or plasterboard down alongside stud to finished floor, Illus. 89. Remove all debris.

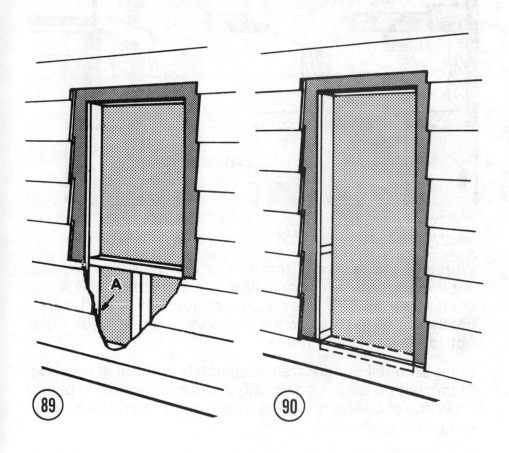

Saw off shoe and sill. If builder neglected to install a jack stud A, under sill, Illus. 90, cut and nail same in place. Cut exterior siding back from opening a distance casing on door frame requires. Only remove siding. Do not remove felt over subsheathing. If builder neglected to cover subsheathing with felt, staple a 9'' wide strip by length required around door opening.

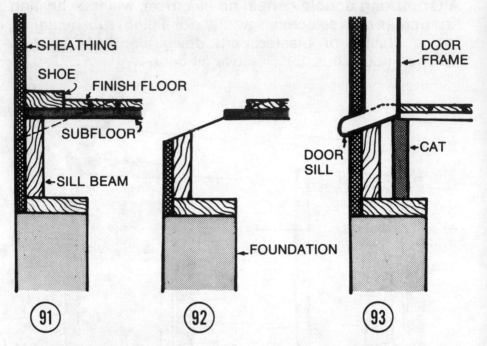

SHEATHING

SHOE

FINISH FLOOR

SUBFLOOR

SILL BEAM

DOOR FRAME

DOOR SILL

CAT

FOUNDATION

91 92 93

Working inside, saw through shoe, finished flooring, subflooring and sill beam, Illus. 91, from zero to 2¼'' or amount sill on new door frame requires, Illus. 92. Using a hatchet or wide chisel, chop sill beam to angle required for outside door sill and frame.

Place an outside door frame, complete with sill in opening. Plumb with a level, horizontally and vertically. When plumb draw line of casing on siding. Remove frame and saw siding to receive casing.

Cut a 2 x 6 or 2 x 8 cat, Illus. 93, to size required. Force in place under cut edge of floor. Nail flooring to cat.

Nail frame in place with 8 penny finishing nails. Drive nails through casings into studs. Countersink heads. Fill holes with wood putty before painting. Calk joint between siding and casing.

TO BUILD A STEP

If patio requires building a step, follow this procedure. Cover clapboard with #15 roofing felt or ½" asphalt impregnated board. Build form to size shown, Illus. 94. Do not drive nails all the way in. Fill with concrete consisting of one part cement, three parts sand to four parts gravel. Allow to set sufficiently so you can score surface. Allow to set three days. Carefully pull nails and remove form.

Mix one part cement to two parts screened sand. Spread a 1" layer of mortar over step and embed a piece of slate or flagstone in position, Illus. 95. Allow flagstone to project ¾" or 1" over front and ends. Finish face of step with mortar consisting of one part cement to two parts of finely screened sand.

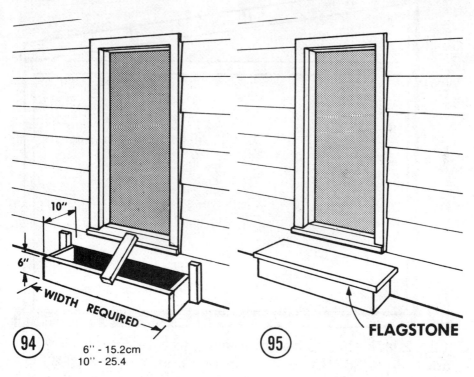

10"

6"

← WIDTH REQUIRED →

94 6" - 15.2cm
10" - 25.4

95 FLAGSTONE

HOW TO SCREEN A PATIO

Those wishing to screen in a patio should tack a 2 x 2 temporarily in position against siding, squarely in line with outside face of corner post, Illus. 96. Check 2 x 2 with level to make certain it's plumb. Check 2 x 2 and corner post with a straight length of 2 x 4 and a square.

When square and plumb, draw lines down both sides of 2 x 2, Illus. 97. Using a handsaw, saw through siding. Using a wide chisel, remove cut siding. Since you will want to screen in the upper area, cut siding to full height required. Use care to only saw through shingle or clapboard, not into #15 felt or subsheathing.

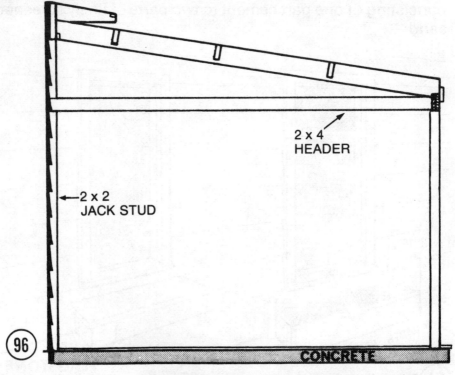

2 x 4 HEADER

2 x 2 JACK STUD

96

CONCRETE

Cut 2 x 2 jack stud to height needed to support a level 2 x 4 header, Illus. 96. Spike 2 x 2 in position. Cut 2 x 4 header exact length required. Toenail to 4 x 4 post and to 2 x 2. Cut a length of 2 x 2 and nail in position above header. Using size nail shingle or clapboard requires, nail cut siding. Calk joint between siding and 2 x 2.

Measure space between jack stud and corner post. Divide by four. Build 1 x 2 screen frames, Illus. 98, to size required. Apply glue before assembling and nailing frame.

Place frames in position. Measure 6" in from end of each frame, Illus. 99. Drill 3/16" holes through 1 x 2 at bottom and top.

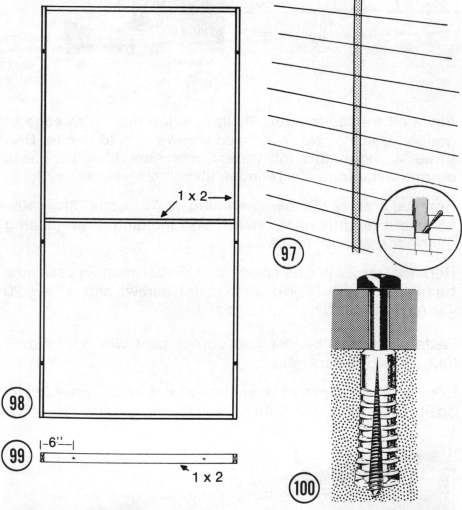

Nick concrete and header to locate exact position of each hole. Number frame and concrete so when you remove frames, each can be accurately repositioned. Using a carbide tipped bit, drill holes in deck to size expansion shield, Illus. 100, or jack nut, Illus. 101, requires.

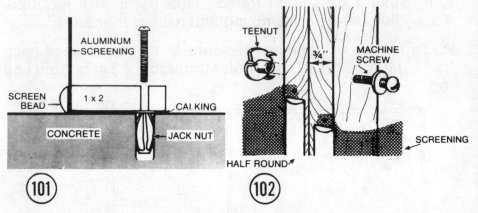

Place all frames temporarily in position flush with edge of header. Use 1½" No. 7 flathead screws to hold frames. Drill three ¼" holes through vertical members, Illus. 98. These permit fastening with Teenuts, Illus. 102.

Remove frames. Staple screening to ¾" edge, Illus. 102. Miter cut lengths of ½" half round molding. Nail molding over edge with 1" brads.

Replace frames in exact position. Vertical members can now be fastened with ¼" No. 20 machine screws and ¼" No. 20 Teenuts, Illus. 102.

Fasten frame to header and corner post with 1½" No. 7 flathead wood screws.

Upper part of patio can be enclosed by stapling screening in position shown. Cover with ½" half round molding, Illus. 103.

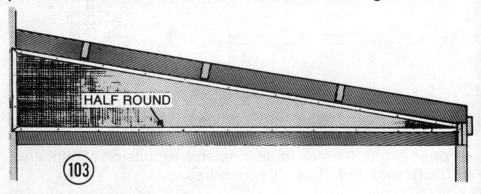

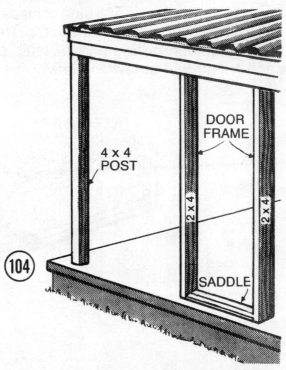

Since many families prefer a completely enclosed patio, an outside screen door is optional. Position same where desired. Frame opening with 2 x 4 posts and header*, Illus. 104. Build screens to size required to fill space available, Illus. 105.

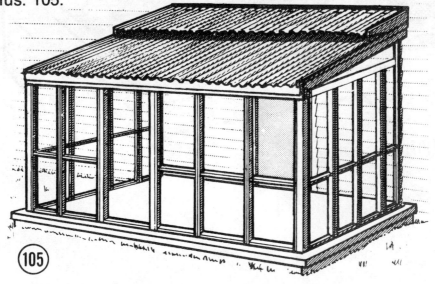

* If required

Screens for air vents should be made to size required, Illus. 106. Nail redwood filler strips to top. These frames should butt snugly against roofing panels, Illus. 107. Drill hole in side of each frame and screw frame to vent rafter.

FILLER STRIP

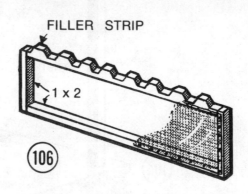

1 x 2

106

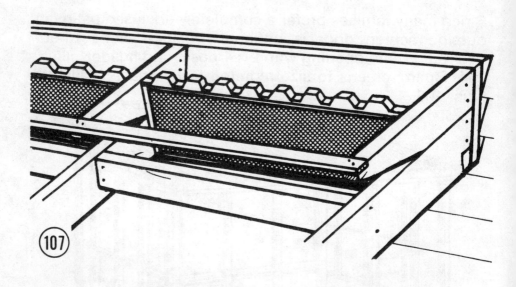

107

HOW TO MAKE ALUMINUM SCREEN FRAMES

Aluminum screen frame extrusions, Illus. 108, available in most home improvement centers, permit assembling screens to any width desired even up to 42". They can be installed vertically or horizontally. Extrusions are available in 6 and 8' lengths complete with splicers and corner locks, Illus. 109. Splicers, Illus. 110, permit joining frame extrusion end to end. A mitered corner, Illus. 111, receives corner lock.

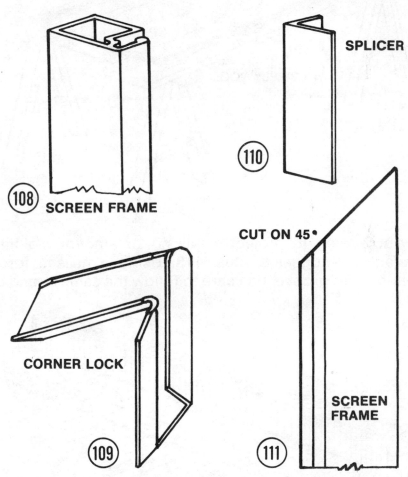

SPLICER

(110)

(108) SCREEN FRAME

CUT ON 45°

CORNER LOCK

(109)

(111)

SCREEN FRAME

Assemble aluminum frames to overall size of opening less 1/8", or thickness of metal required to hold frame in position at top, sides, center and bottom.

To simplify assembling large aluminum screen frames, make a jig, Illus. 112. Tack two 2 x 6 or 2 x 8 to saw horses. Space planks distance required. Cut ¼ x 2'' strips of plywood to length required to hold frame securely in position. Use 1 x 2 spacers cut to length required. Cut aluminum 45° angle, to length required. Insert mitered corner, Illus. 109.

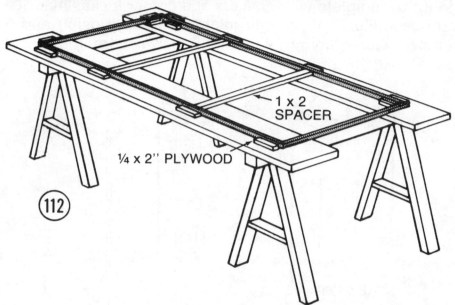

1 x 2 SPACER

¼ x 2'' PLYWOOD

112

Allow screening to project a full ½'' or amount molding manufacturer suggests, Illus. 113. Using a nailset, force screening into groove. Use care to follow the same strand of wire.

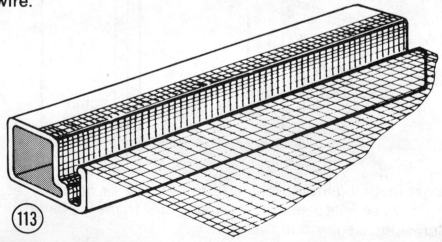

113

Insert spline in position, Illus. 114, across top. Tack two ¼ x 2" blocks at bottom to hold frame in position. Pull screening taut. When splines have been inserted all around, cut waste wire close to spline.

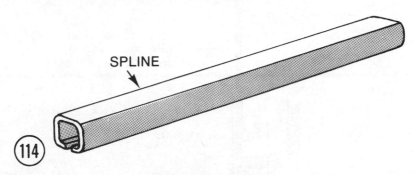

SPLINE

(114)

Cut ½ x ½ or 1 x 1" angle to length required to hold screens in place. Notch corners, Illus. 115.

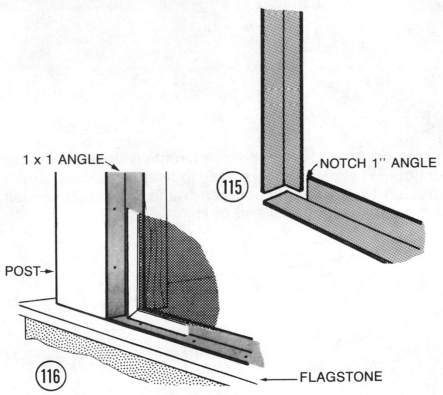

1 x 1 ANGLE

NOTCH 1" ANGLE

(115)

POST→

(116)

FLAGSTONE

Screw angle flush with face of post and header, Illus. 116.

Drive jack nut or expansion shield in concrete. Drill holes through bottom angle and fasten angle to deck, Illus. 117. Drill holes through screen frame and angle and bolt frame to angle.

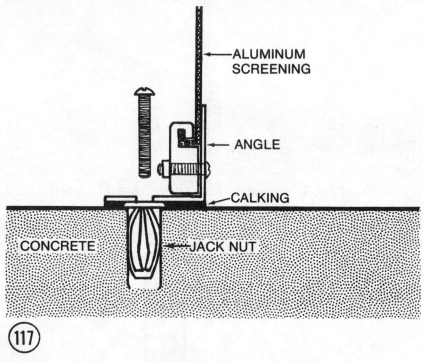

ALUMINUM
SCREENING

ANGLE

CALKING

CONCRETE   JACK NUT

(117)

To connect two screens either horizontally or vertically, cut aluminum H extrusion, Illus. 118, to length required. Buy H extrusion to size that fits screen frame. To butt H section flush against angle, saw end of H.

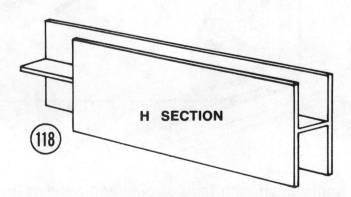

H SECTION

(118)

Insert screen in H section, drill holes, bolt H to screen frame. Place assembled screen in place and bolt angle to frame, Illus. 119. Always dip each bolt in vaseline. Come the day a screen needs replacement, the nut will be removable.

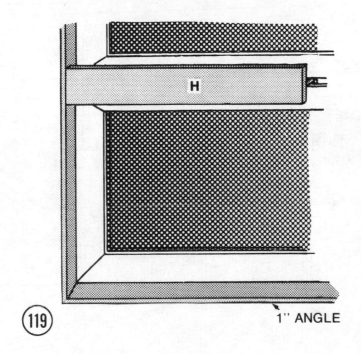

119 1" ANGLE

HOW TO BUILD A PORCH OR CARPORT WITH A SUNDECK ABOVE

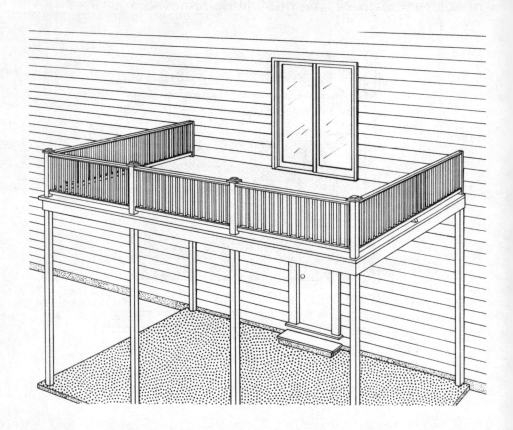

The growing need for singles housing, plus the incredible cost of housing for an aging parent, have triggered a boom in turning a second floor bedroom or two into a separate apartment. When a porch or carport is constructed with a second story sundeck, it adds outdoor living space that greatly enhances a rental unit. This is especially attractive to those faced with an aging parent housing problem. The cost of all material is minimal compared to nursing home bills.

A foundation for a 12 x 16' porch or 12 x 20 or 24' carport, Illus. 120, follows procedure described for a patio with these exceptions. A porch or carport requires ⅝ or ¾" plywood roof sheathing. Place 2x6 rafters and ceiling joists every 16".

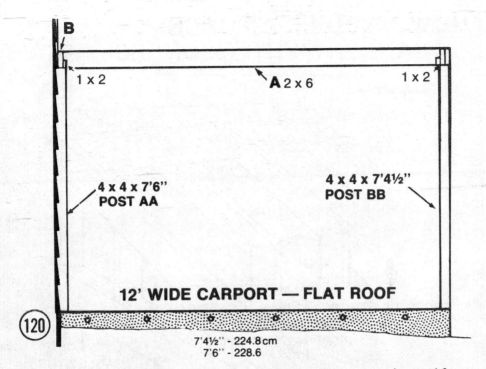

B

1 x 2

A 2 x 6

1 x 2

4 x 4 x 7'6"
POST AA

4 x 4 x 7'4½"
POST BB

12' WIDE CARPORT — FLAT ROOF

(120)

7'4½" - 224.8 cm
7'6" - 228.6

Allow 6 x 6 reinforcing wire to project over area selected for a ramp. Embed wire in concrete ramp.

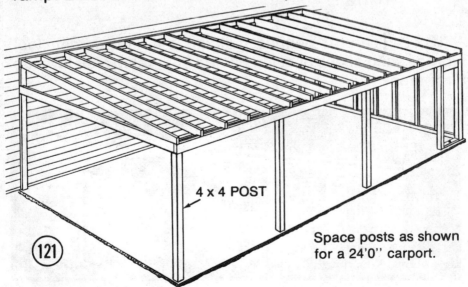

4 x 4 POST

(121)

Space posts as shown
for a 24'0" carport.

Those building a carport without a sundeck, Illus. 121, should stiffen rafters with 1 x 6 truss ties, gable studs, and joists, Illus. 121a.

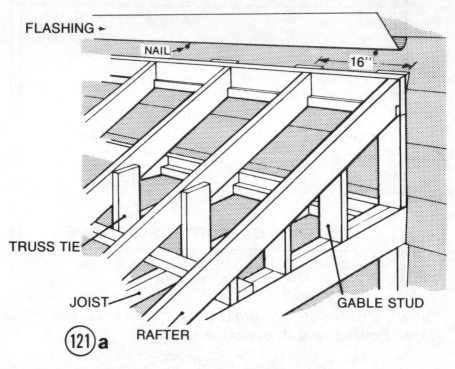

16'' - 40.6 cm

FLASHING ←

NAIL

16''

TRUSS TIE

JOIST

RAFTER

GABLE STUD

(121) a

A 12 x 24' carport permits building a 4 x 12' garden tool storage shed at one end, Illus. 121b. Pour ramp after leveling floor area.

(121) b

While a porch or carport roof can be framed with the same rafter used for the patio, Illus. 49, a "flat roof" permits use as a second story sundeck. 2 x 6 or 2 x 8 joists should be cut to provide ⅛" pitch to the foot. This totals 1½" in 12'. If post AA is 7'6", post BB, Illus. 120, will be 7'4½". Note directions on page 42, 56.

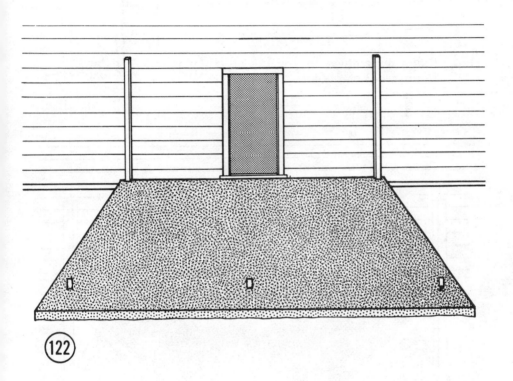

(122)

2 x 6 framing for ABCD, Illus. 126, is acceptable by most codes. Use 2 x 8 where snow loads, and/or codes require same.

12 x 16' is an ideal size for a porch, 12 x 20 or 12 x 24' for a carport. Pour slab, embed post anchor straps. Temporarily nail two 2 x 4's against house at spacing desired, Illus. 122. Check with level to make certain each is plumb. Follow directions previously described to saw through thick butt of clapboard, Illus. 123, 124. Remove 2 x 4's.

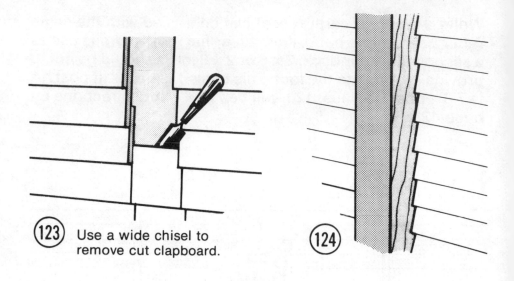

(123) Use a wide chisel to remove cut clapboard.

(124)

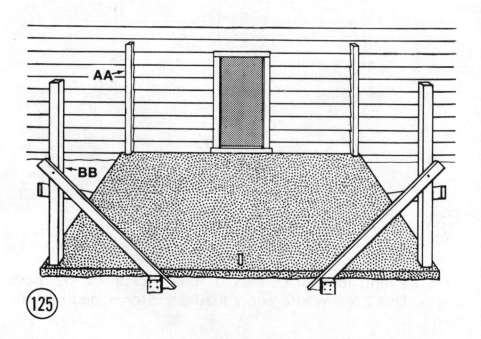

AA

BB

(125)

Cut two 4 x 4 posts 7'6'', Illus. 125, two 7'4½''. Apply wood preservative. When dry, apply a coat of exterior paint. When dry, spike 7'6'' posts in position to house with 16 penny nails. Countersink heads. Fill holes with wood filler. Renail siding alongside posts. Calk joint, Illus. 125.

78

Raise, plumb and brace outside posts in position, Illus. 125.

Cut two 2 x 6 x 15'9'' B* for a 16' wide porch. Nail 1 x 2, Illus. 52. Nail one 2 x 6 B in position across top of posts against house, Illus. 126. If conditions warrant using 2 x 8 for joists G, use same size lumber for ABCD.

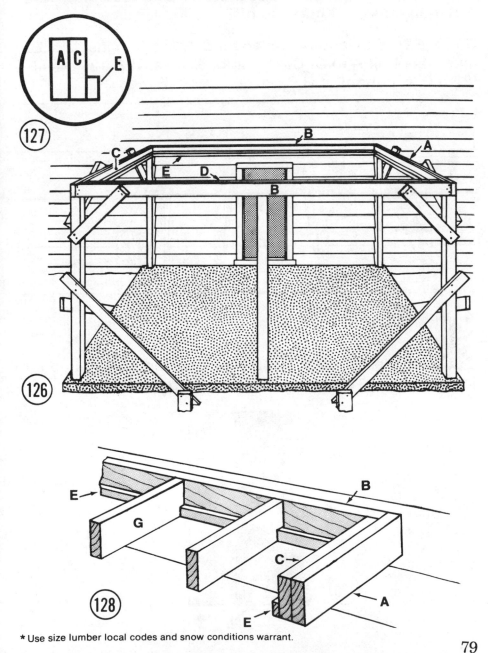

* Use size lumber local codes and snow conditions warrant.

Cut two 2 x 6 x 12', or length required for A. Nail A to end of B, Illus. 128. A finishes flush with outside face of post. Check assembled frame to make certain it's square. Brace in position.

Cut two 2 x 6 by length needed for C. Nail C to A, Illus. 127, 128. Nail outside B into end of C.

Cut one 2 x 6 to length needed for D. Spike D to inside of B, Illus. 126. Nail A to D. Cut 1 x 2 for E, Illus. 127, 129. Nail E flush with bottom of B,C,D.

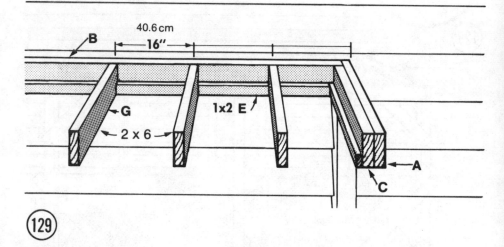

Cut eleven lengths 2 x 6 x 12' to overall length required for joists G, Illus. 129, 130. Notch ends to receive E.

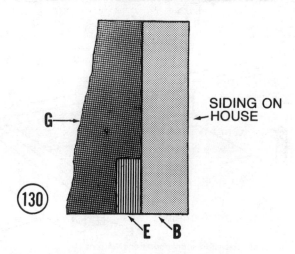

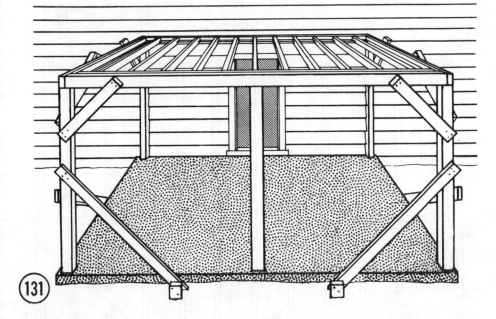

(131)

Toenail joists 16" on centers to B and D, Illus. 131. Nail 2 x 6 cats or steel bridging in position shown, Illus. 132, 133. Nail fascia in position, Illus. 134. Use a 1 x 8 for 2 x 6 joists, 1 x 10 for 2 x 8 joists.

Nail ⅝ or ¾" exterior grade plywood sheathing to roof, Illus. 134. Use 8 penny common nails. Space panels ⅛" apart to allow for expansion. Sheathing finishes flush with fascia.

Install copper or aluminum flashing, Illus. 134, under first course of siding that is 1" or more above deck. Use width flashing needed to slide 3" under clapboard and still project 3" plus over deck.

Using a hammer and nailset, drive siding nails through clapboard. Using width flashing needed, cut to length required. Slide 3" under clapboard and renail siding so nails only go through top edge of flashing. Bend flashing up slightly.

Roof can be covered with canvas, plastic coatings or built up roofing. Apply with adhesive manufacturer recommends. After roofing is completed, nail flashing to deck keeping nails along outside edge.

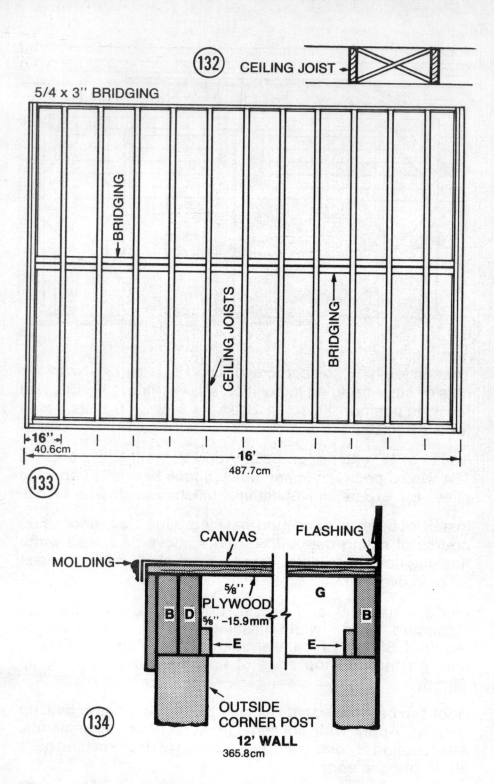

(132) CEILING JOIST

5/4 x 3" BRIDGING

BRIDGING

CEILING JOISTS

BRIDGING

16"
40.6cm

16'
487.7cm

(133)

CANVAS   FLASHING

MOLDING→

5/8"
PLYWOOD
5/8" −15.9mm

B D   G   B

E   E

OUTSIDE
CORNER POST

(134)

12' WALL
365.8cm

82

A built up roofing isn't difficult to lay. Book #696 Roofing Repairs Simplified covers the job step by step. Those who plan on using the roof area should protect same with a slatted deck, Illus. 135. Nail 1 x 2 to 1 x 2. Space slats ¾" apart. Make up 4 x 4 sections. This permits easy handling.

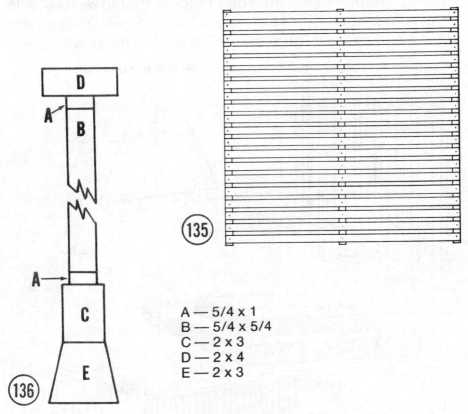

A — 5/4 x 1
B — 5/4 x 5/4
C — 2 x 3
D — 2 x 4
E — 2 x 3

The sundeck should be enclosed with railings. This can be a prefabricated wood or metal railing, or build one, Illus. 121. Use 4 x 4 x 32" outside corner posts. Cut posts longer if you want a higher railing. Position outside posts 3" from corners. Fasten in place with 3" angle brackets. Cut pickets 22¼" for 31" railing. Use materials specified, Illus. 136. Using a piece of 2 x 4 as a spacer, space pickets 3½" apart.

Cut top and bottom rail A, Illus. 136, from 5/4 x 1" to length required to extend from corner post to house. Cut pickets to length required. Apply glue and nail A to each B, except those against house and post. Use 8 penny finishing nails.

Cut four 2 x 3 spacer blocks E to size and shape shown, Illus. 137. Position E at center. Toenail C to E. Place assembled railing in position against corner post. Check with level. When level and plumb, draw line on post and on house to indicate bottom of rail A. Apply glue, plumb and nail a picket to post, another to house. Top of picket should be level with drawn line. Apply glue to picket. Nail A to picket. Toenail A to house and to post. Countersink heads. Fill holes with putty.

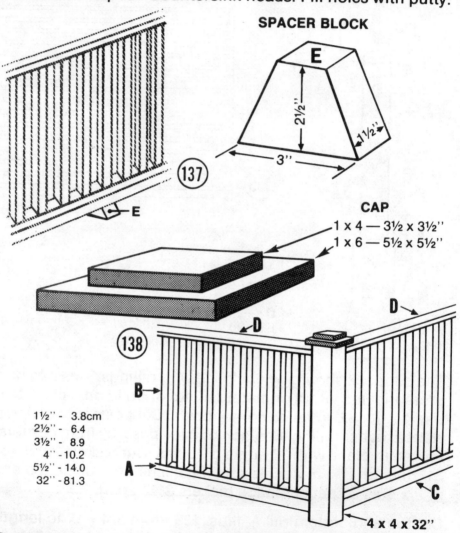

SPACER BLOCK

2½" 1½" 3"

137

E

CAP

1 x 4 — 3½ x 3½"
1 x 6 — 5½ x 5½"

D

138

B

D

1½" - 3.8cm
2½" - 6.4
3½" - 8.9
4" - 10.2
5½" - 14.0
32" - 81.3

A

C

4 x 4 x 32"

Cut 3½ x 3½" corner caps from 1 x 4; 5½ x 5½" from 1 x 6, Illus. 138. Apply glue and nail 5½ x 5½" to post. Apply glue and nail 3½ x 3½" in position. Use 6 penny finishing nails.

BUILD A PORCH ON POSTS

(139)

Those needing to replace a back porch usually have to build on posts, Illus. 139. These can be 4 x 4 wood, Illus. 140, or 6'' poured concrete piers, Illus. 141. The posts should be cut to height required to support framing BC, Illus. 141, 142.

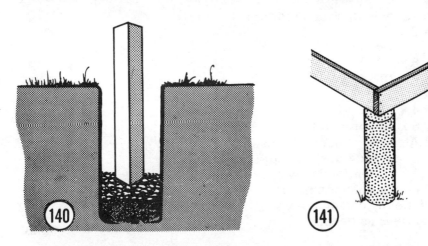

(140)   (141)

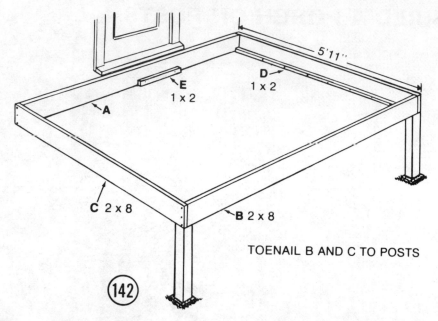

5'11"

E
1 x 2

D
1 x 2

A

C 2 x 8

B 2 x 8

TOENAIL B AND C TO POSTS

(142)

To replace an existing porch, remove steps and broken concrete foundation. For a 6'0'' x 8'0'' porch, Illus. 143, 144, erect batter boards, level up guide lines and check diagonals. 4 x 4 wood posts are shown in Illus. 143. Location of 6'' concrete forms is shown in Illus. 144a.

LIST OF MATERIALS — 6 x 8' Porch, Illus. 139.

2 — 2 x 8 x 8' - A,B
1 — 2 x 8 x 12' - C
1 — 1 x 2 x 14' - D,E
5 — 2 x 6 x 8' - F,G,H
1 — 2 x 12 by length required for K
3 — 2 x 3 x 8' - L
2 — 2 x 8 x 12' - M
6 — 2 x 6 x 12' - N
5 — 2 x 4 x 10' - Q,S,U,V
1 — 2 x 4 x 8' - R
1 — 2 x 4 x 8' - T
2 — 2 x 6 x 12' for stair treads (4 treads)
OPTIONAL — 6'' concrete forms
              4 x 4 posts - length required
              Reinforcing wire or ½'' reinforcing rods
3 lbs. 8 penny common nails
3 lbs. 16 penny common nails
finishing nails as needed

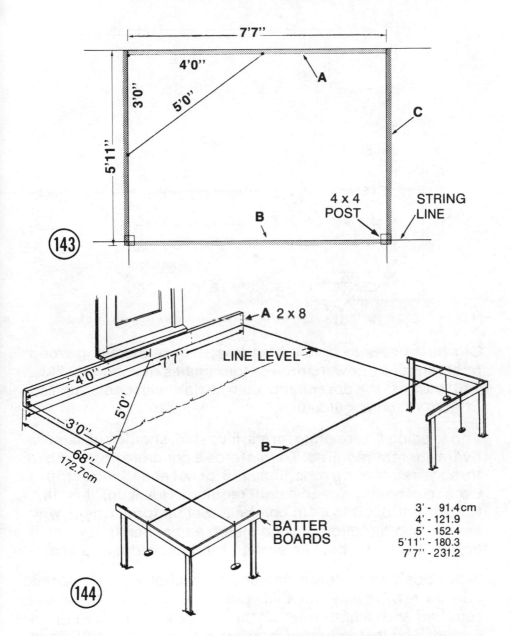

7'7"

4'0"

3'0"

5'0"

5'11"

A

C

B

4 x 4
POST

STRING
LINE

(143)

A 2 x 8

LINE LEVEL

7'7"

4'0"

5'0"

3'0"

68"
172.7cm

B

BATTER
BOARDS

3' - 91.4cm
4' - 121.9
5' - 152.4
5'11" - 180.3
7'7" - 231.2

(144)

Cut 2 x 8 A, 7'7", Illus. 144. Check with level. Nail in position 2 or 7" below door sill with 16 penny nails. Drive nails into studs.

Erect batter boards level to height equal to bottom of A. For a floor pitch of 1" in 6'0" width of porch, make a 1" saw cut in batter boards and drop lines 1".

87

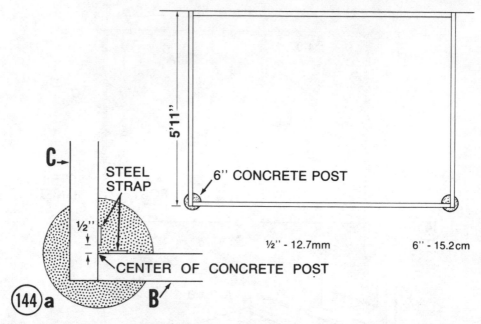

C→

STEEL
STRAP

½"

5'11"

6" CONCRETE POST

CENTER OF CONCRETE POST

½" - 12.7mm   6" - 15.2cm

(144)a   B↗

Dig post holes to below frost level. Those installing wood posts should throw in three or four inches of concrete, Illus. 140, position the post plumb, then fill hole with concrete. Top of post touches guide line.

Those using 6" concrete forms, Illus. 145, should cut same to overall height required. To reinforce a concrete post, embed three 1" reinforcing rods, Illus. 146, or cut an 11" wide strip of 6 x 6 reinforcing wire to height required. Roll it up, Illus. 147. Embed bottom 3 to 4" in concrete. Set up form. Check with level in two directions. When plumb and at height level with line B, Illus. 144, backfill around form to hold it in place.

Since positioning forms and setting anchor straps in forms can be a bit tricky, do this. Cut 2 x 8 C and B to length required and temporarily nail them in position to A. Support C and B with temporary bracing placed about 4'0" from house. Check diagonals. Make certain CB slopes to provide 1" pitch in 6'0". You can now position post or form exactly where it's needed. You can also estimate where to embed the anchor strap. You can proceed to permanently anchor a wood post or fill the concrete form or remove C and B, then proceed.

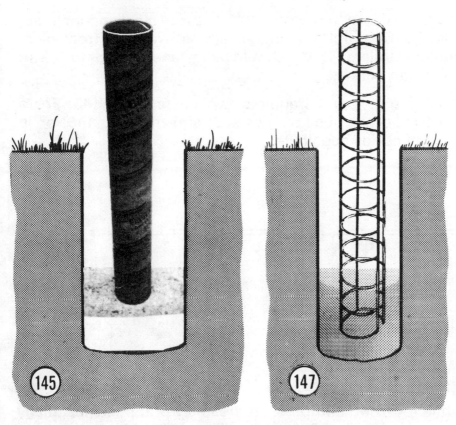

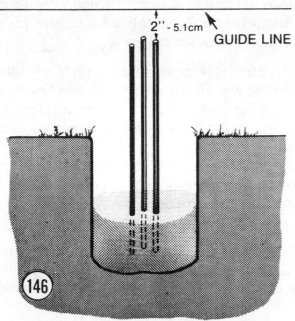

2'' - 5.1cm

GUIDE LINE

89

Drill ¼" holes in 3/16 x 1 x 12" lengths of steel anchor strap, Illus. 24, or purchase anchor straps available from most lumber retailers. These should be fastened to B or to C with ¼ x 2" lag screws.

A 6'0" x 8'0" porch requires two posts, Illus. 143. For a 12 x 20' porch, position posts as shown, Illus. 148, or in position codes specify.

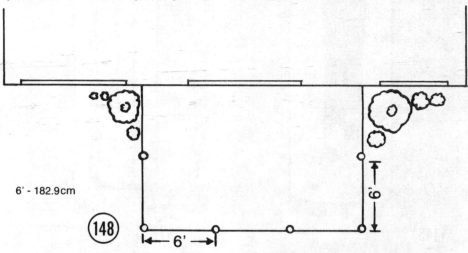

6' - 182.9cm

6'

148

6'

While redwood and pressure treated wood posts last many years, they do rot. Concrete posts provide better construction. Use 6" diameter concrete tubes for columns up to 4'0", 8" diameter tubes for taller columns.

Those erecting concrete posts should fill form with a 1-3-4* or 1-3-5 mix on the wet side. Use a 1 x 2 or ½" reinforcing rod to puddle concrete down around reinforcing. Embed anchor strap in position required. Allow forms to set undisturbed for three days before stripping form or framing. Set an electric saw to cut ¼" or thickness of form. Make two cuts, then remove form. In cold weather, use Hydro-Set or other anti-freezing agent when mixing concrete. Protect form against a freeze up.

Cut 2 x 8 B same length as A, Illus. 142. Cut two 2 x 8 to length required for C. Cut ends of C at angle required to finish flush with B. Spike C to A and to B. Check corners to make certain it's square.

*One part cement, three parts sand, four parts gravel

Cut two 1 x 2 x 5'8" or length required for D, Illus. 142. Since a 1 x 2 measures 1½", a 2 x 6 — 5½", a 2 x 8 — 7¼", if you nail a 1 x 2 to C, ¼" up from bottom edge, 2 x 6 F will finish flush with top of C, Illus. 149.

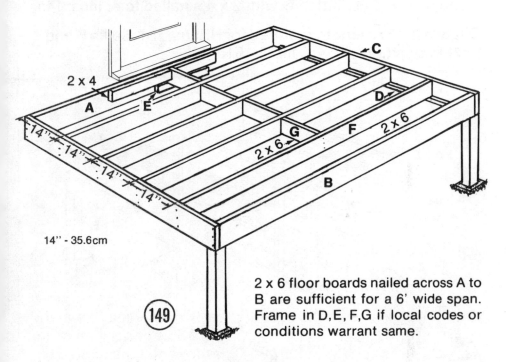

14" - 35.6cm

2 x 6 floor boards nailed across A to B are sufficient for a 6' wide span. Frame in D,E,F,G if local codes or conditions warrant same.

Nail 1 x 2 x 12" E to A in position shown ¼" up from bottom edge of A, Illus. 150. Nail 2 - 2 x 4's to A in position shown, Illus. 149, 150.

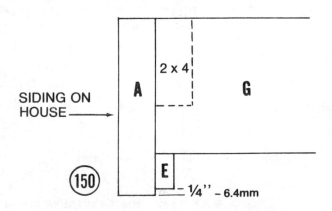

SIDING ON HOUSE

¼" – 6.4mm

Cut four 2 x 6 to length required for F, Illus. 149. Nail C to F with 16 penny nails.

Cut four 2 x 6 G to length required. Toenail G to A against house with 8 penny nails. Stagger others so you can nail through F into G. Stiffen G with 2 x 4's nailed to A, Illus. 149.

Cut two 2 x 6 to length required for H, Illus. 151. Spike B and F to H in position shown, Illus. 151a.

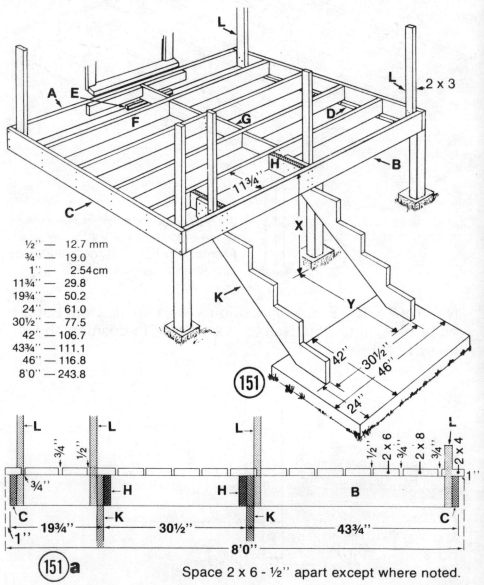

½" —	12.7 mm
¾" —	19.0
1" —	2.54cm
11¾" —	29.8
19¾" —	50.2
24" —	61.0
30½" —	77.5
42" —	106.7
43¾" —	111.1
46" —	116.8
8'0" —	243.8

Space 2 x 6 - ½" apart except where noted.

BUILD STAIRS

Cut two 2 x 12 for K, Illus. 151, 152. To determine number of steps required, location and height of slab at base of steps, follow this procedure. Measure from grade at base of post to top edge of B, distance X, Illus. 151.

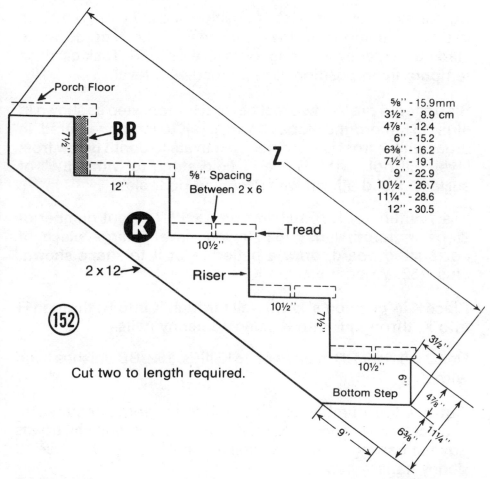

Cut two to length required.

Divide X by 7½" to ascertain number of risers. Any balance left over in the event X does not divide evenly indicates height slab should be built above grade.

For example: If X measures 40", and you divide by 7½", the answer is 5 risers with 2½" left over. This assumes floor of porch as a step. The number of treads is equal to the number of risers, less one tread (the porch floor).

To establish dimension Y, multiply the number of treads by 10½".

To establish Z, length of carriage, Illus. 152, count number of steps (5 - including porch as one), multiply by approximately 13".

Set form for concrete slab in position and at height required. In this installation the slab would be 2½" above grade. Make slab 46" wide, by 42" long, or to size desired. Tack carriage temporarily in position. Check tread with level.

Slab should project two feet beyond bottom step as shown in Illus. 151. If ground slopes down, cut K to length required. In areas where frost is a problem, excavate to depth below frost level. Fill hole with rubble or field stone to within 5½" of surface. Build a form with 2 x 6 and pour slab.

Draw outline of K to full size on 2 x 12. Lay out number of steps required, Illus. 152. If you have a large piece of corrugated board, draw a pattern. Cut it to shape shown, Illus. 152. When it fits, cut K.

Place K in position shown. Nail through K into H; through H into K; through B into K using 16 penny nails.

Nail 2 x 8 riser BB in position to K, Illus. 152. BB finishes flush with K.

Cut needed number of 2 x 6 treads to length required to project 1" over edge of K, Illus. 152, 153. Butt and nail treads against carriage. Allow ⅝" spacing between treads. Use 16 penny nails.

Cut six 2 x 3 x 41¼" posts L. Saw 1 x 2 D off at corners to allow L to be fastened flush with bottom edge of C and B. Paint with wood preservative. Nail or bolt to inside of C in position shown, Illus. 151, with 16 penny nails.

Cut 2 x 4 for R. Cut R to shape shown, Illus. 154, to receive Q on left and on right. Cut to length required.

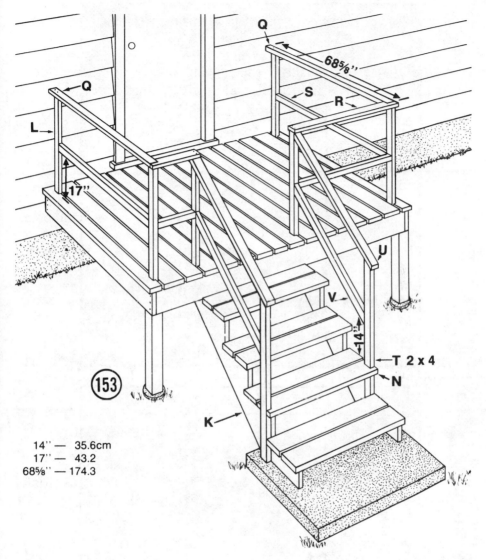

(153)

14" — 35.6cm
17" — 43.2
68⅝" — 174.3

Cut two 2 x 4 for Q to length required. Check Q and R with level and nail through Q into L. Nail through R into L. Drill hole through edge of R and drive a 16 penny nail into end of Q.

Cut 2 x 4 S to length required. Nail in position shown with 8 penny nails, Illus. 153. S is nailed flush with L.

Cut two 2 x 4 x 47" posts T* to angle shown on pattern, Illus. 155. Notch step N to receive T, Illus. 153.

Nail T to K and N with 10 penny nails.

*Cut T to height your stairs require.

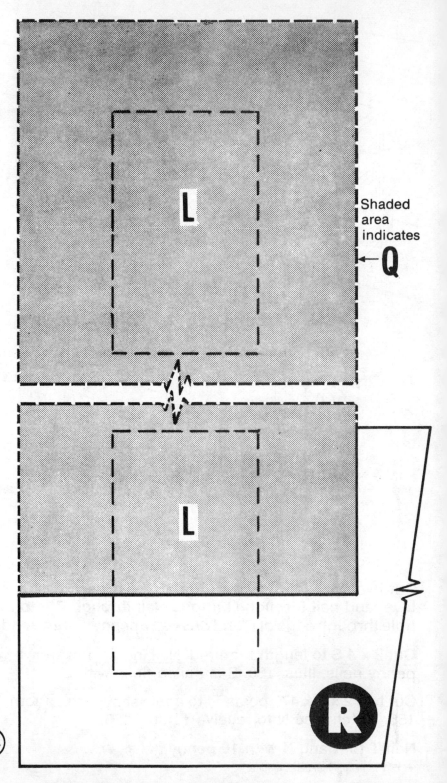

Shaded
area
indicates
← **Q**

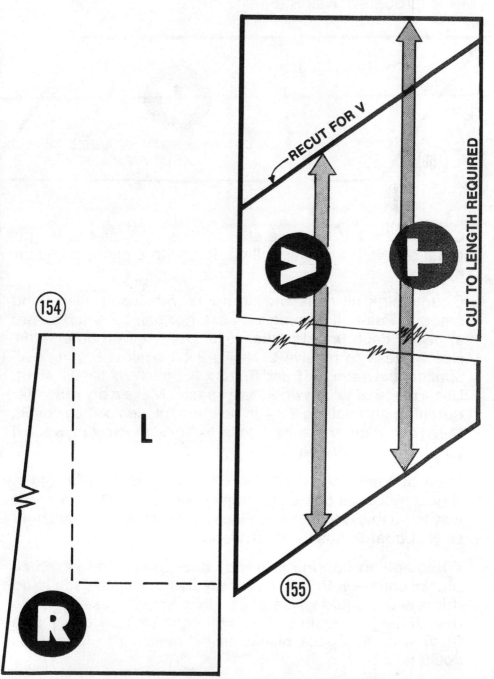

Cut two 2 x 4 U to angle shown, Illus. 156, and to length required. Allow U to overhang T 2 to 4''. Place in position. Drill pilot holes through U to permit nailing U to T and L. Drill hole through R. Nail R to U.

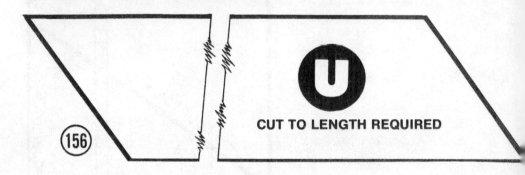

CUT TO LENGTH REQUIRED

(156)

Cut two 2 x 4 V to angle shown, Illus. 155, and to length required. Nail in position, Illus. 153, with 8 penny common nails.

Countersink all nails and fill holes with wood filler. Sand smooth. Paint all framing with exterior paint or stain before applying deck boards, Illus. 151a. Use 2 x 4 on outer ends. Notch these to receive L. Nail a 2 x 8 against L. Allow ¾'' spacing between 2 x 8 and first 2 x 6. Space 2 x 6's ½'' apart. Use a piece of ½'' plywood as a spacer. Make a dry run. After notching and nailing 2 x 4 in position, place 2 x 8 against L, then lay out other planks. Use ¾, ⅝ or ⅜'' piece of plywood if you have to alter spacing.

Many builders use a 2 x 4, 2 x 6, 2 x 8 pattern, Illus. 160, then repeat. Allow all boards to project over C and B 1''. An easy way to do this is to tack two pieces of ½'' plywood over C and B. Nail boards flush with plywood.

When nailing flooring to a wide deck, use care to keep all planks square with frame. An easy way for one person to do this is with a square, Illus. 160a. Make a square using 1 x 4 to overall length required. Select straight 1 x 4's. Keep 4' side flush with A. Space planks using pieces of plywood as spacers.

98

A single box beam, B, C, Illus. 151, is sufficient for a porch. Use a double 2 x 8 for B, C, on a larger deck, Illus. 157, 158. Space double C members every 6 to 8'0" or distance codes specify. If you are building an 8, 10 or 12' wide sundeck, add framing D,F,G, Illus. 149, on spans exceeding 6'0". Use 8" diameter concrete form for piers. Roll up a 14' wide length of 6 x 6 wire reinforcing, Illus. 147, for an 8" tube. Embed two anchor straps, Illus. 159.

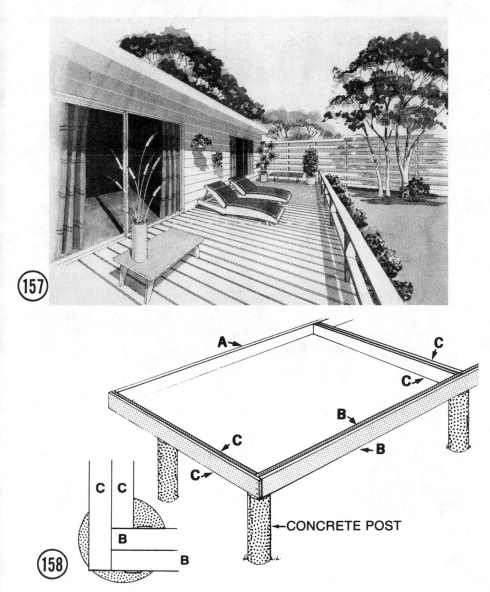

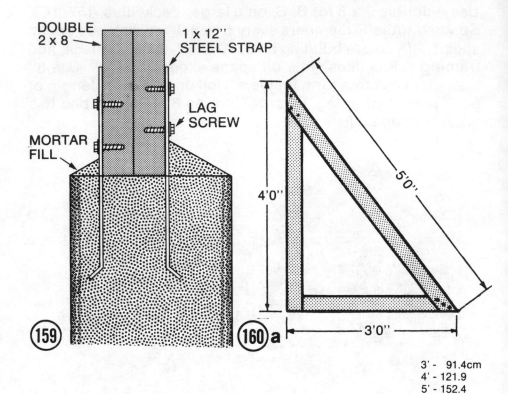

DOUBLE 2 x 8

1 x 12" STEEL STRAP

LAG SCREW

MORTAR FILL

159

160 **a**

4'0"

5'0"

3'0"

3' - 91.4cm
4' - 121.9
5' - 152.4

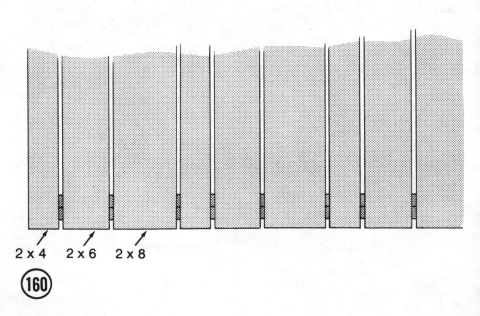

2 x 4   2 x 6   2 x 8

160

When flooring over a raised foundation frame, for an enclosed porch, a solid wood floor can be nailed in place. Use single or double tongue and groove, 1½ to 2½" thick western red cedar, Illus. 161. This makes an excellent, long wearing deck. Plane tongue off starting plank. Position planed edge 1½" over edge of C and B.

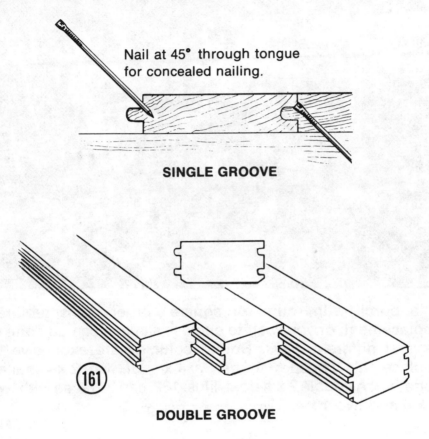

Nail at 45° through tongue for concealed nailing.

SINGLE GROOVE

DOUBLE GROOVE

CONSTRUCTION AGAINST
CONCRETE BLOCK AND BRICK FACED HOUSES

When building a porch or sundeck against a concrete block or brick faced wall, drill holes in masonry using a carbide tipped bit. Use size that permits installing expansion shields, Illus. 56, 101, in masonry. Fasten A, Illus. 141, in position with 2½ to 3" lag screws.

HOW TO ENCLOSE A PORCH

If a porch with round or square corner posts requires replacement, or you wish to enclose same, it can be done in several different ways. Round columns are expensive to replace. It's cheaper to use a 4 x 4 or two 2 x 4 nailed together. A double 2 x 4 post, Illus. 162, can be faced with two 1 x 6 and two 1 x 4.

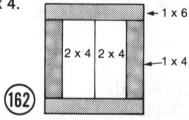

To remove an existing load bearing corner post, cut a 4 x 4 or double 2 x 4 to length required to support plate level. Using a car jack, take the load off existing corner column. Position new post in exact position as existing one. Don't raise plate any higher than necessary.

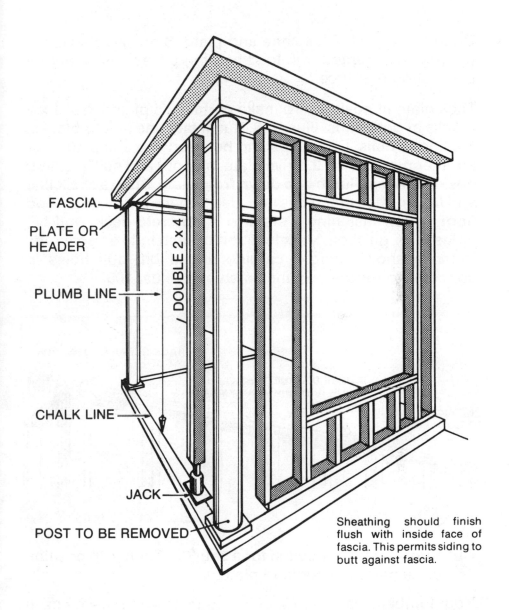

FASCIA

PLATE OR HEADER

PLUMB LINE

DOUBLE 2 x 4

CHALK LINE

JACK

POST TO BE REMOVED

Sheathing should finish flush with inside face of fascia. This permits siding to butt against fascia.

To enclose a porch, drop a plumb bob down from inside face of fascia. Snap a chalk line. Measure ⅜'' for ⅜'' sheathing, ½'' for ½'' sheathing and snap a line. Frame in wall to this line. Apply sheathing and siding.

By positioning wall frame ⅜, ½ or ⅝'' (thickness of sheathing) in from chalk line, it allows for clapboard siding to butt against fascia.

Build frame with 2 x 4 shoe and plate. Since most existing porches are framed with load bearing plates, a single 2 x 4 plate should suffice.

Tack plate in position. To make certain it's plumb, nail 1 x 2 blocks at both ends, Illus. 163. Run a taut line across blocks. Tie line to nails. Check spacing between line and plate with another piece of 1 x 2. Drive plate in or out and nail in plumb position. Drop plumb bob down from plate. Snap a chalk line and fasten shoe along this line. Use 16 penny nails on a wood floor. When fastening a shoe to a concrete deck, drill ¼" holes through shoe. Mark location of each hole on concrete. Remove shoe. Using a carbide tipped bit, drill holes in concrete to receive expansion shields, Illus. 100.

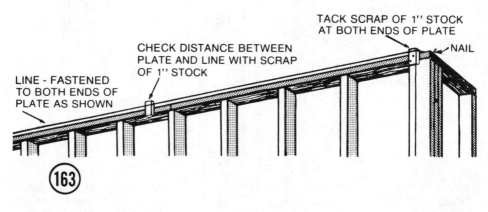

TACK SCRAP OF 1" STOCK AT BOTH ENDS OF PLATE

NAIL

CHECK DISTANCE BETWEEN PLATE AND LINE WITH SCRAP OF 1" STOCK

LINE - FASTENED TO BOTH ENDS OF PLATE AS SHOWN

163

Cut studs to length needed for a snug fit. Toenail in position 16" on centers to shoe and plate.

Your lumber retailer will specify rough opening size for each window and door you select. He will need to know how you plan on finishing the interior and exterior in order to provide window and/or door casings to fit. If you decide to nail ½" gypsum board to interior walls, then apply ¼" paneling to studs, ⅝" sheathing outside, he needs to know. Illus. 164 shows cutaway of a wall. With this information, he can deliver windows and gliding doors with proper size casings. Illus. 165 shows a typical window installation.

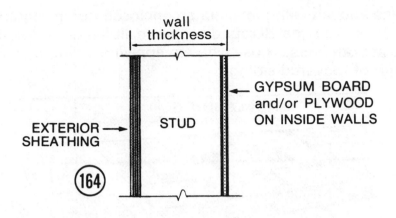

wall thickness

GYPSUM BOARD
and/or PLYWOOD
ON INSIDE WALLS

STUD

EXTERIOR
SHEATHING

(164)

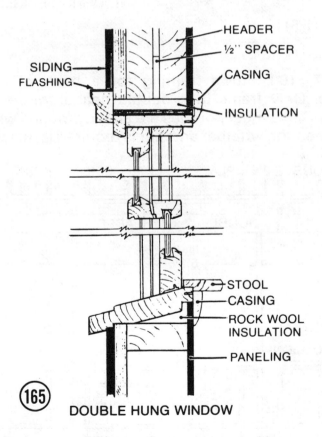

HEADER
½" SPACER

SIDING
FLASHING

CASING

INSULATION

STOOL
CASING
ROCK WOOL
INSULATION

PANELING

(165)
DOUBLE HUNG WINDOW

Always space a double header with pieces of ½" plywood so header equals width of stud.

Space above ceiling joists in an enclosed porch requires a free flow of air. Install round or square aluminum vents, Illus. 166, at both ends. Those who are applying siding can use a length of louvered siding.

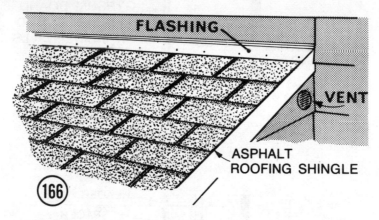

FLASHING

VENT

ASPHALT
ROOFING SHINGLE

166

Illus. 167, 168 shows framing for a bank of casement windows. Only frame in a double header where same is required. Since most porches are already framed with a load bearing header, whether another is required is questionable.

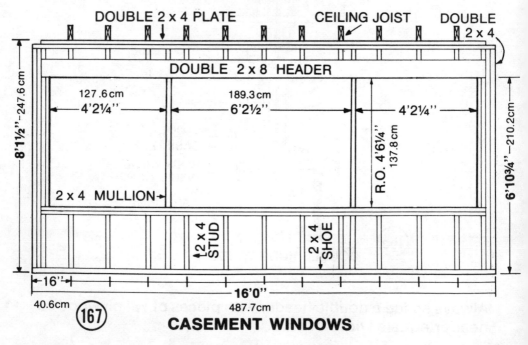

DOUBLE 2 x 4 PLATE   CEILING JOIST   DOUBLE 2 x 4

DOUBLE 2 x 8 HEADER

8'1½"–247.6 cm

127.6cm
4'2¼"

189.3cm
6'2½"

4'2¼"

R.O. 4'6¼"
137.8cm

6'10¾"–210.2cm

2 x 4 MULLION→

2 x 4 STUD

2 x 4 SHOE

16"
40.6cm

16'0"
487.7cm

167

CASEMENT WINDOWS

While Illus. 167 shows a single 2 x 4 mullion, some codes may require two. Always space studs below sill 16" on centers. Use jack studs alongside windows and below sill.

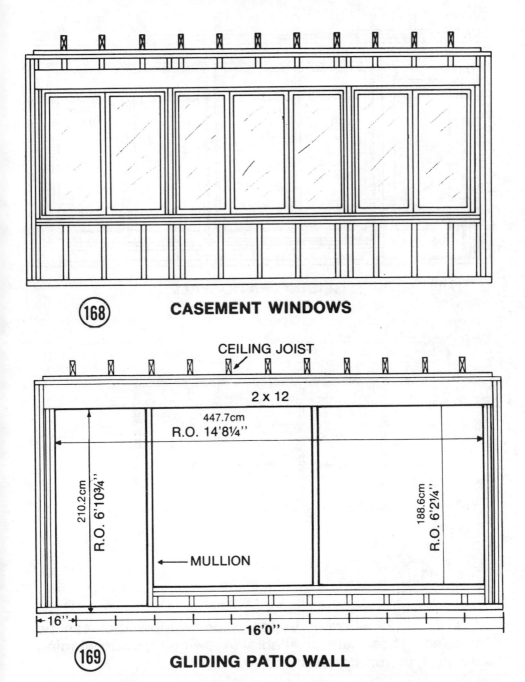

(168) **CASEMENT WINDOWS**

CEILING JOIST

2 x 12

447.7cm
R.O. 14'8¼"

210.2cm
R.O. 6'10¾"

188.6cm
R.O. 6'2¼"

← MULLION

16" 16'0"

(169) **GLIDING PATIO WALL**

Framing for gliding glass doors is shown, Illus. 167, 170.

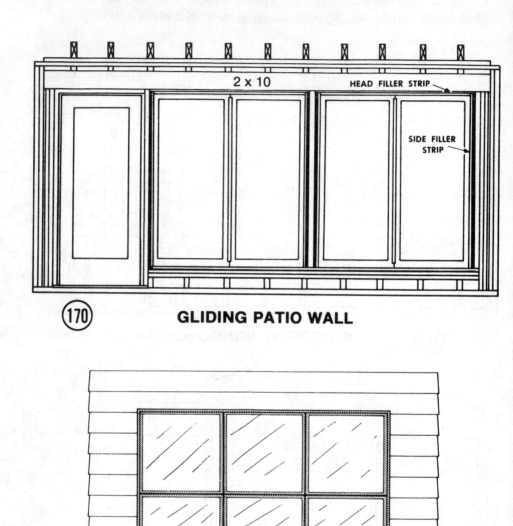

2 x 10   HEAD FILLER STRIP

SIDE FILLER STRIP

⑰ **GLIDING PATIO WALL**

⑰

Illus. 171, 172 show a hopper type window that can be installed. These are available in swinging, outswinging awning type, or stationary.

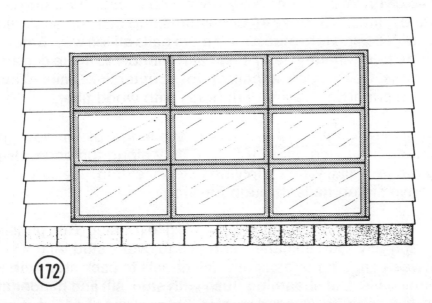

(172)

When more than one window is to be installed in a rough opening, toenail each temporarily in plumb position. Don't drive nails all the way until all windows are placed in position.

(173)

Check with level. If necessary, shim with shingle. Working on outside, Illus. l73, drive 10 penny finishing nails on an angle through casing into stud. Don't drive nails all the way. Before nailing permanently, test open each window to make certain it works freely. Use a nailset to countersink nails. This prevents marring casing. Fill holes with wood filler.

Install aluminum flashing along top edge of window in position indicated, Illus. 165. Nail only along top edge. Use aluminum nails. When applying exterior siding, use care not to drive siding nails through flashing.

Nail ⅜, ½, ⅝ or ¾" plywood sheathing to framing. Run panels horizontally. Butt all panels end to end over a stud. Allow ⅛" between ends for expansion. Nail panels to each stud with 8 penny nails. Cut sheathing flush with stud, sill and header at window opening. Cut and staple 9" wide strips of #15 roofing felt around each window and door opening, Illus. 173.

While most quality windows are prime coated before delivery, prime coat same immediately if it wasn't done at the factory.

Read directions window manufacturer provides. Some recommend an additional coat of paint before installation. Use care to keep paint off weatherstripping and hardware.

When enclosing a porch against a brick or stucco faced house, position end stud as close as possible, then calk joint. Calk joint between a shoe and a concrete floor. If necessary, use shingle to level shoe. In this case, grout joint with a mortar consisting of one part cement to three parts of finely screened sand.

NOTE: While gliding doors are most frequently installed in an outside wall, many are also used between a completely enclosed porch and adjacent room. If you decide to install same, brace ceiling joists, Illus. 174, to take the full load off outside wall.

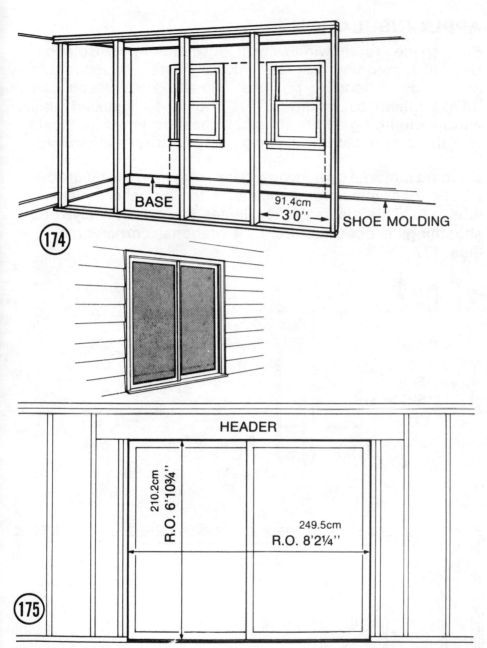

BASE

91.4cm
←3'0"→

SHOE MOLDING

(174)

HEADER

210.2cm
R.O. 6'10¾"

249.5cm
R.O. 8'2¼"

(175)

Cut opening to width and height required to frame opening with a double header of sufficient size to support the load, Illus. 175. Frame opening to size retailer suggests. Your retailer can suggest size of header depending on size of doors ordered.

APPLY INSULATION

Pack space around window with loose rock wool insulation. Use full or medium thick rock wool blankets between rafters and studs depending on local climate. Your dealer can advise thickness required. This should be installed after wiring, plumbing and heating have been roughed in. Staple to rafters and studs following manufacturer's directions.

Building material dealers now sell 8' long tongue and groove plastic foam insulation panels that can be nailed to studs, Illus. 176. This insulation eliminates the need for plywood sheathing. It does require 1 x 4 diagonal corner bracing, Illus. 177.

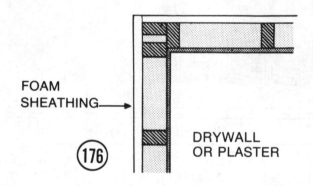

FOAM
SHEATHING——►

DRYWALL
OR PLASTER

(176)

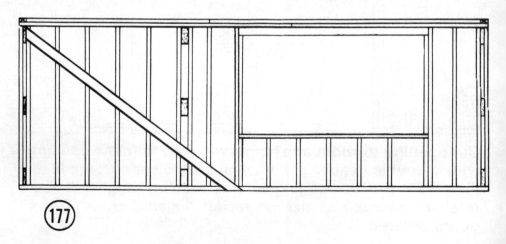

(177)

Place 1 x 4 by length required diagonally across studs. Draw lines where brace crosses each stud. Remove brace and notch stud, Illus. 178, to receive full thickness of 1 x 4. Nail brace to each stud using two 8 penny common nails. The foam panels are nailed with big head roofing nails. Use size, and space nails, following foam manufacturer's recommendations.

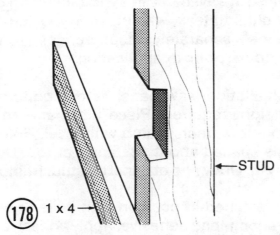

←—STUD

(178) 1 x 4 —←

When enclosing a porch, make every effort to insulate a raised foundation. Apply plastic foam insulation, Illus. 179, to inside. If this isn't accessible, apply it to outside of wall. Plastic foam insulation comes in ¾, 1, 1½ to 2'' thick. Use thickness dealer recommends for weather in your area. Foam should cover foundation down to footing. Nail foam to sill beam with big head roofing nails. Foam can be bonded to foundation block with mastic adhesive manufacturer recommends. Do not use asphalt cement.

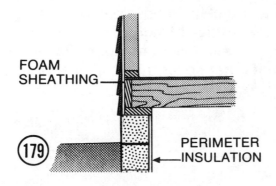

FOAM
SHEATHING—

(179)

PERIMETER
←—INSULATION

INSTALL CEILING, INTERIOR PANELING

After all electrical work, and where needed, heating has been roughed in, apply ½" gypsum board or acoustical tile to ceiling, ¼" hardboard or hardwood plywood to walls. Interior paneling comes in 3/16 and ¼" thickness, 4 x 7 and 4 x 8' size. Place panels in porch to condition them prior to installation. These are available in a wide selection of natural wood grains including teak, walnut, cherry, oak, pecan and birch. Stand panels separately on long edges around room for at least 48 hours prior to application.

To simplify installation, saw panel across bottom ¼" less than overall height required. Place first panel in position against ceiling and corner. Plumb with level. Hold in place with three nails spaced about 12" apart at top. Don't drive nails all the way in. Draw line of panel on stud. Remove panel.

Panels can be fastened in position with nails or with panel adhesive. We recommend adhesive. Apply adhesive with gun type applicator ⅛" thick to studding and other framing members. Replace panel in plumb position with same three nails. Press panel in place. Using nails as a hinge, pull panel from wall at bottom and prop it 6 to 8" away from wall. Allow adhesive to get tacky. Depending on heat and humidity, this usually takes 8 to 10 minutes. When adhesive becomes tacky, press panel firmly in position. Using a padded block of wood and a hammer, apply pressure along line of adhesive. Nails at top may now be removed and holes filled with Putty Stik. If any adhesive appears on surface, clean up with naphtha or white gasoline as quickly as possible. A cartridge of panel adhesive contains sufficient adhesive to apply four to six 4 x 8 panels. Book #605 How to Apply Paneling contains many helpful hints that cover many special problems.

HOW TO TRIM A CASEMENT WINDOW

Illus. 180 shows position of inside trim. Remove two screws holding casement window opener to temporary block support. Remove opener, knock off block. Both head and side filler strips supplied by window manufacturer should be cut width required to finish flush with face of interior paneling. Nail head filler strip, then side strip in position with 8 or 10 penny finishing nails. Temporarily nail two blocks in position to support sill level.

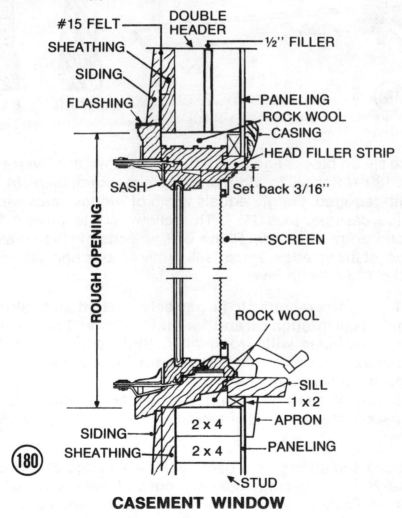

CASEMENT WINDOW

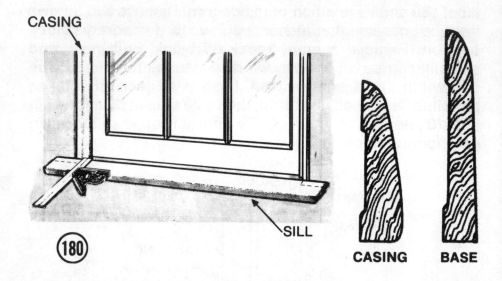

CASING

SILL

(180)

CASING   BASE

Place sill on blocks and with square, mark width of window, Illus. 180. Notch sill to width and depth required; then cut sill length required. Length equals width of window, plus width of side casings, plus 1½". This allows sill to project ¾" beyond edge of casing. Plane or saw ends of sill to match shape of front edge. Press sill firmly in position. Remove blocks. Check with level.

Cut 1 x 2 to size required to fill gap between bottom of sill and framing. Nail through sill and 1 x 2 into framing. Countersink heads. Fill holes with wood filler. Stuff loose rock wool insulation. Cut molding to length required for apron. Length of apron equals width of window plus casings. Nail apron in position snug against sill. Butt a length of matching molding against sill. Measure and miter cut to length required for side casing.

Side and top casing sets back 3/16" from edge of window frame. Nail side casing. Measure, cut and nail top casing in position. Fasten opener in position using screws previously removed. A matching base molding is also available. Nail in position after installing finished flooring.

SIDING SIMPLIFIED

Apply exterior siding to match that on your house or use vinyl, aluminum, prefinished plywood or hardboard siding, Illus. 181. Codes in many areas now permit nailing siding directly to studs spaced 16" on centers. If codes require sheathing, use plywood to thickness required. If no sheathing is used, your dealer will suggest installation procedure for siding he sells.

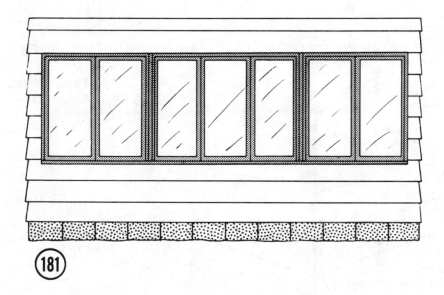

(181)

Staple #15 roofing felt horizontally across sheathing (or across studs if no sheathing is used). Allow felt to overlap each course about 4".

Your siding dealer sells prefinished metal inside and outside corners, Illus. 182. When applying siding to a wall that butts against existing siding, Illus. 183, use 5/4 x 5/4 for an inside corner. Place 5/4 x 5/4 in corner over existing siding. Draw a line. Saw siding width required to receive 5/4 corner board. Nail 5/4 x 5/4 corner in position. Renail siding. Calk joints.

When applying siding to adjoining walls, use metal inside corner, Illus. 182. These can be nailed in position with 5 penny box head galvanized nails.

117

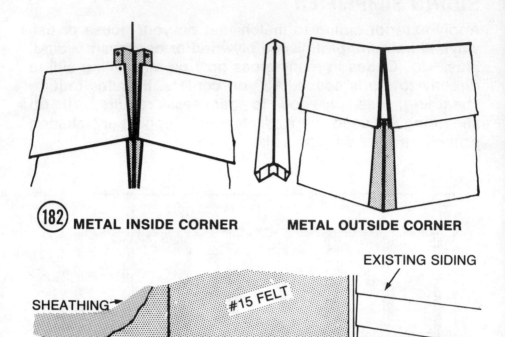

182 **METAL INSIDE CORNER**   **METAL OUTSIDE CORNER**

EXISTING SIDING

SHEATHING

#15 FELT

STARTER STRIP

5/4 x 5/4"

SIDING OUTSIDE CORNER

INSIDE CORNER

183

An experienced siding applicator divides space from top of window to foundation by the width of clapboard. To make certain a course of siding is level with top of window, he marks each course off on a 1 x 2 siding pole. This helps establish location for first course, Illus. 183, 184. Snap a chalk line and nail metal starter strip, available from your dealer, in position with 5 penny 1¾" galvanized siding or box nails. If necessary, starter strip can be fastened up to 1" below edge of sheathing. You can also cut a course of siding to fit. Allow ⅛" gap between edge of siding and window sill, and between end of siding and a door or window casing. Calk joint.

118

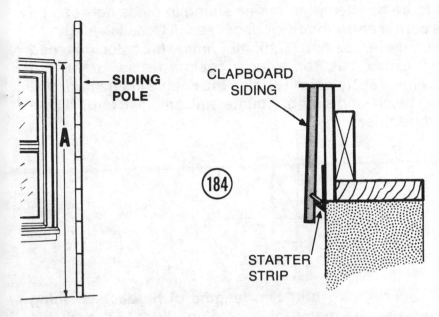

SIDING POLE

CLAPBOARD SIDING

(184)

STARTER STRIP

If conditions permit using metal inside corner, nail same in position. Hold siding in position and drive 8 penny galvanized box head nails into each stud. Drive nails ½" from top edge of siding.

Don't countersink heads of siding nails unless siding manufacturer specifies same. The heads create a gap that helps vent siding, Illus. 185.

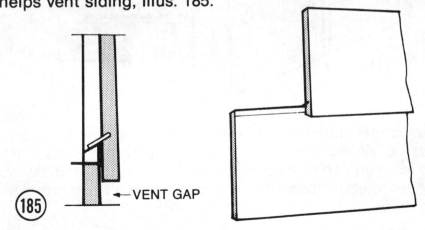

(185) ←VENT GAP

Tabs on outside corners slide under and are covered by siding. Nail corner in position with an 8 penny nail at top, Illus. 182.

Don't force or attempt to spring siding in place between an inside corner and window or door casing. Cut each length so it fits freely in position. Calk all joints with color matched calking. Either butt top course against fascia, or fur out fascia, Illus. 186, to permit sliding top course in position. Nail through fascia and siding. Countersink nailhead and fill hole with wood filler.

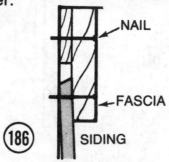

NAIL

FASCIA

(186) SIDING

When necessary to butt two lengths of hardboard siding together, use the metal joint molding, Illus. 187, available from your siding retailer.

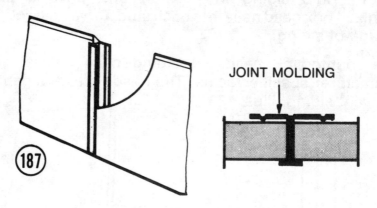

(187)

JOINT MOLDING

When codes permit siding without plywood sheathing, butt ends of siding over a stud. Where sheathing has been applied, you can butt ends anywhere necessary, but always stagger joints so two adjoining courses don't butt one over one.

Nail siding 16" on centers. When nailing over doors and windows, use care not to nail through flashing except along the top edge, Illus. 188.

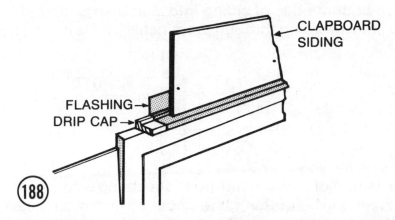

CLAPBOARD
SIDING

FLASHING→
DRIP CAP→

(188)

Hardboard siding comes in 12' lengths and is packed 72 sq. ft. to a bundle. A 72 sq. ft. bundle covers 60.4 square feet with 10 13/16'' exposure. This includes 5% for waste when cutting.

ADDITIONAL SIDING FACTS

Since there are many different kinds of clapboard siding and each requires application according to manufacturer's directions, it's necessary to read and follow same.

The following steps of application apply to insulated aluminum siding. Nail a level 1 x 2 for starter strip, Illus. 183, at height width of siding requires to allow a course to line up with top of window. Nail 1 x 2 starter strip level with bottom of sheathing or it can project as much as 1'' below.

Nail metal starter strip to 1 x 2, Illus. 189. Recess starter strip distance from corner siding manufacturer suggests.

1 x 2 —

(189)   (190)

If you use a circular saw, Illus. 190, to cut siding, use goggles and a blade manufacturer suggests. Cut siding to overall length required, less ¼''. This allows ⅛'' for an expansion joint at each end.

Lock bottom edge of siding into starter strip, Illus. 191. Nail top edge of siding through prepunched holes into each stud.

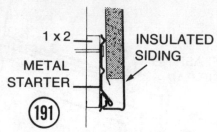

1 x 2

METAL
STARTER

INSULATED
SIDING

(191)

Nail length of beveled furring to sheathing where a cut piece of clapboard requires same under a window sill, eave, etc. Nail preformed undersill in position, Illus. 192. Cut siding to width undersill requires.

Use a calking gun, Illus. 193, to calk joints before nailing undersill in position.

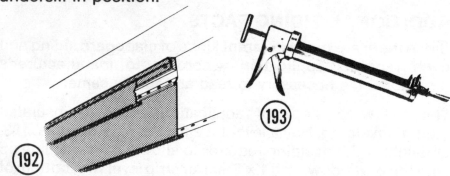

(192)

(193)

Always slip each panel into the lock strip on previous panel, Illus. 194, before nailing along top edge.

Cut window head flashing, Illus. 195, to width of casing plus ½''. This permits bending ¼'' over side. Apply calking before nailing head flashing in position.

WINDOW HEAD
FLASHING

(194)

(195)

SIDE
FLASHING

Always remember to cut clapboard to overall length required less ¼'' to allow for ⅛'' expansion joint at both ends.

THE EXPOSED PORCH RAFTER

Through the years, construction of porches went through many changes. Some had narrow tongue and grooved ceiling boards. Even more were open to the rafters with random spaced joists or ties.

For porch spans up to 12', use 2 x 6 for ceiling joists. Check local codes and use size required. If outside plate is too low, nail joists to rafters at height required, Illus. 196.

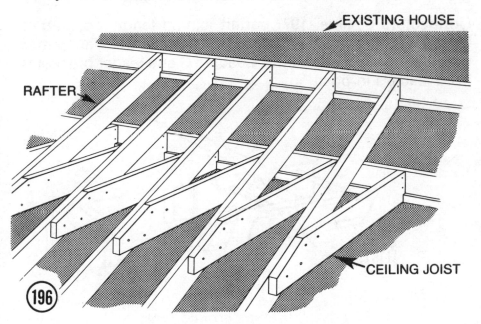

EXISTING HOUSE

RAFTER

CEILING JOIST

(196)

Space joists 16" on centers. Staple insulation between joists and rafters before applying ceiling panels.

The area above joists should be vented with vents, Illus. 166. These can be 3, 4 or 5" diameter. Size is determined by area to be vented. Place at least two at opposite ends of area to create a free flow of air. Aluminum vents are available in various shapes and sizes. Tell your retailer the overall size, length, width and approximate height, and he will select size best suited.

If existing joists or tie beams are spaced at random distance, do not remove same until you have nailed those required.

APPLY CEILING

Use ⅜" exterior plywood for ceiling. Nail in position every 4" along edges, every 6" elsewhere. Finish with ½ or ¾" quarter round.

GUTTERS AND LEADERS

Gutter brackets F, Illus. 197, should be nailed in position every 32, 48 or 60", following directions manufacturer of gutter recommends, before applying shingles.

Connectors C, Illus. 197, permit joining lengths of gutter. These, as well as ends A, should be calked with sealant gutter manufacturer recommends. Leaders G and leader bracket H hold leaders in position.

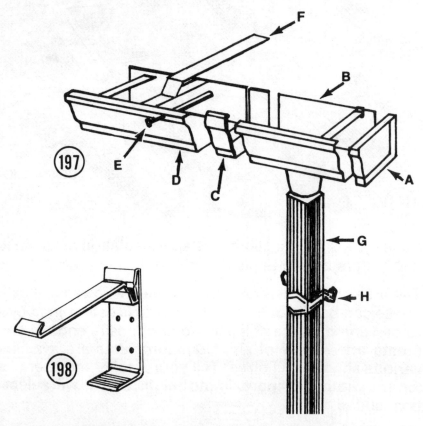

Or you can install gutters using fascia brackets, Illus. 198. These are nailed to fascia.

Another method of installing gutters is with 7'' aluminum spikes and ferrules, Illus. 199. The spike goes clear through from the leading edge of the gutter through the ferrule and back edge into fascia. The ferrule prevents buckling the gutter.

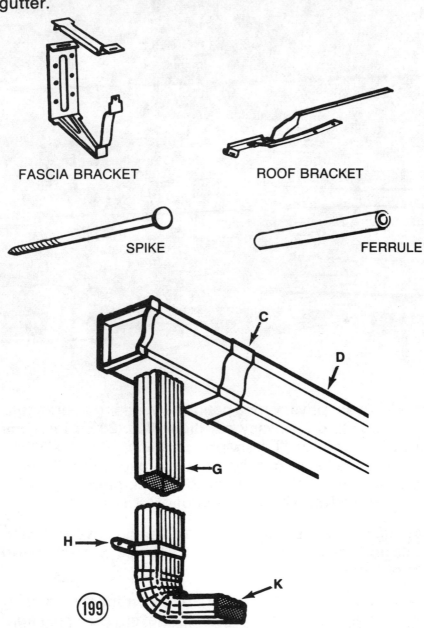

FASCIA BRACKET

ROOF BRACKET

SPIKE

FERRULE

PRIVACY PARTITION

Those who want privacy for a patio or swimming pool should consider building a privacy partition, Illus. 200. Directions suggest building an "L" shaped partition 10 x 20 x 6'3½" high. Any other size can be built by following the same procedure. After cutting lumber to length, prime coat with wood preservative, then one coat of exterior paint.

Directions suggest spacing posts 10' apart. Drive stakes to indicate position of partition. Stretch a line between stakes to locate position of posts.

To make an accurate 90° corner, follow directions on page 23. Dig post holes to depth below frost level. Use a post hole digger.

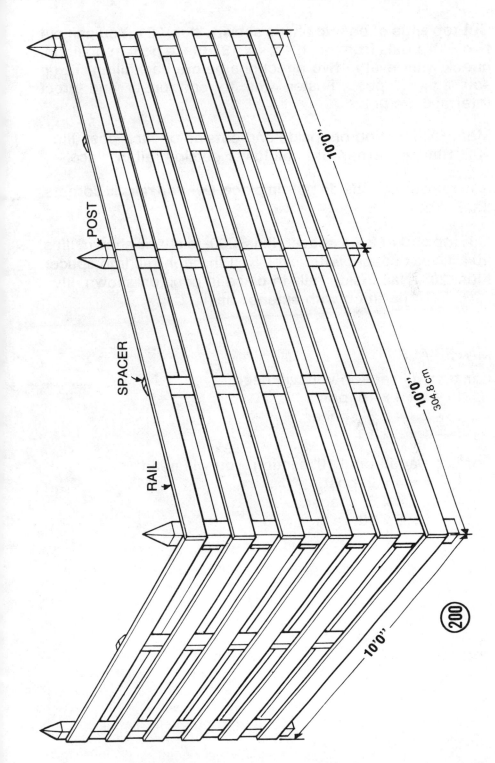

POST

SPACER

RAIL

10'0"

10'0"
304.8 cm

10'0"

200

127

Cut top ends of post to shape shown, Illus. 201. You can cut two 9'0" posts from each 4 x 4 x 18'. Place post in position, check with level in two directions before backfilling. Tamp soil against post. Fasten line to end posts and erect intermediate posts.

Mark rail location on inside and outside of each post, Illus. 202. Start at corner and nail lower outside rail in place.

Nail remaining outside rails in place. Overlap rails at corners, Illus. 203.

Cut top end of 2 x 4 spacer, Illus. 200, to shape shown, Illus. 204. Check spacer with level. Nail through rail into spacer, Illus. 205. Nail inside rails in place in position shown, Illus. 202. Paint partition with exterior paint.

MATERIALS

For first 10' section you will need:
    1 — 4 x 4 x 18' posts
    1 — 2 x 4 x 6' spacer
   11 — 1 x 6 x 10' rails

For each additional 10' section, you will need:
    1 — 4 x 4 x 9' post
    1 — 2 x 4 x 6' spacer
   11 — 1 x 6 x 10' rails

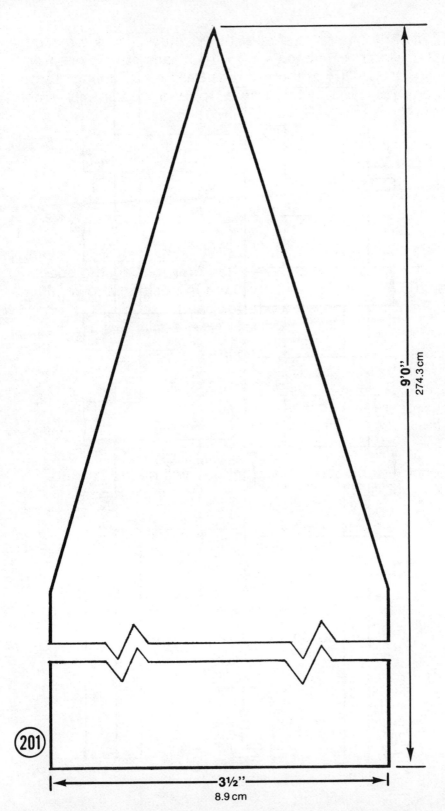

9'0"
274.3 cm

201

3½"
8.9 cm

129

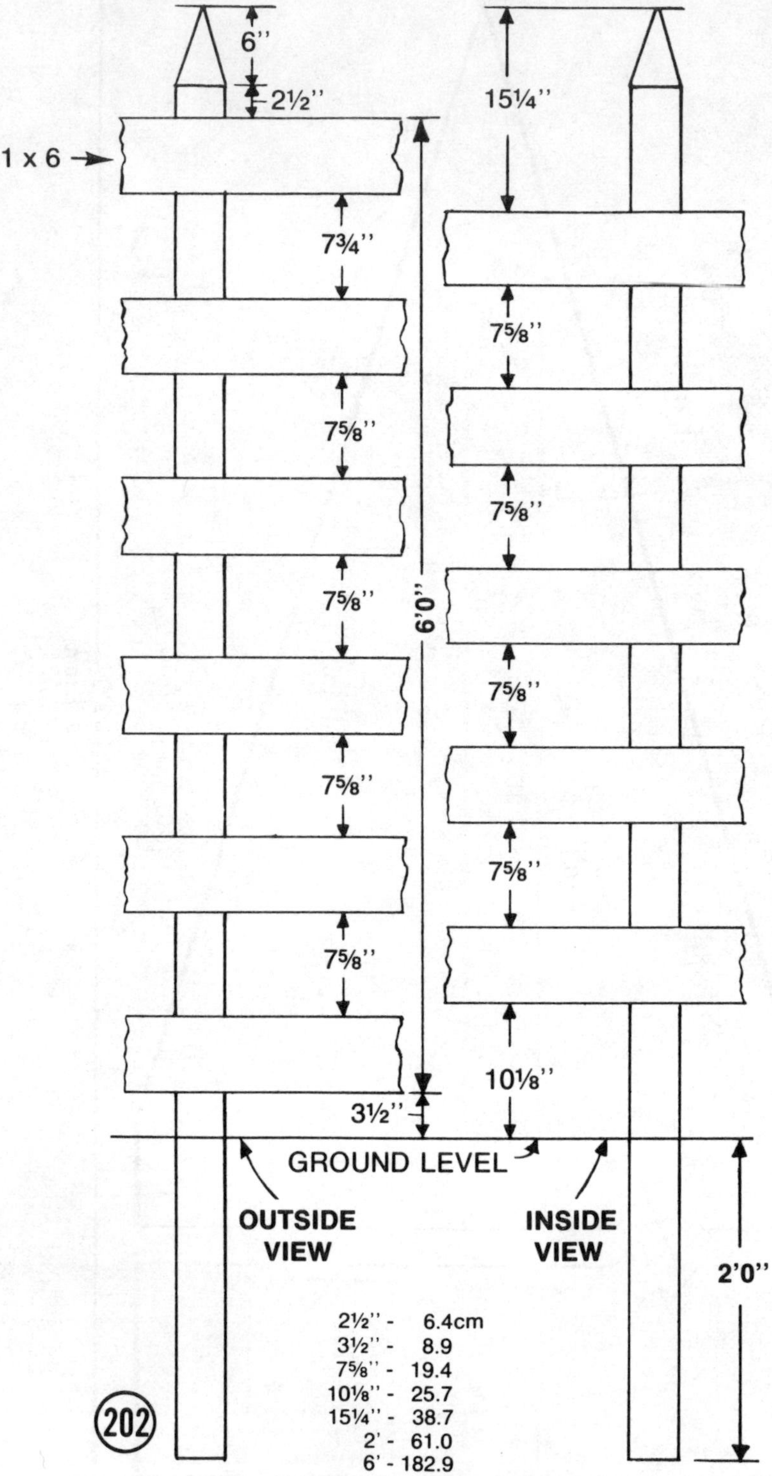

6''
2½''
1 x 6
15¼''
7¾''
7⅝''
7⅝''
7⅝''
7⅝''
7⅝''
7⅝''
7⅝''
7⅝''
6'0''
10⅛''
3½''
GROUND LEVEL
OUTSIDE VIEW
INSIDE VIEW
2'0''

2½'' -	6.4cm
3½'' -	8.9
7⅝'' -	19.4
10⅛'' -	25.7
15¼'' -	38.7
2' -	61.0
6' -	182.9

202

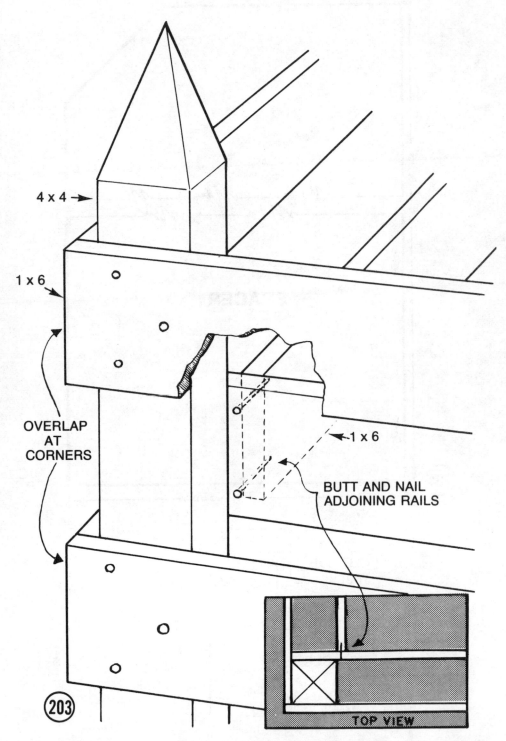

4 x 4 →

1 x 6

OVERLAP
AT
CORNERS

←1 x 6

BUTT AND NAIL
ADJOINING RAILS

(203)

TOP VIEW

131

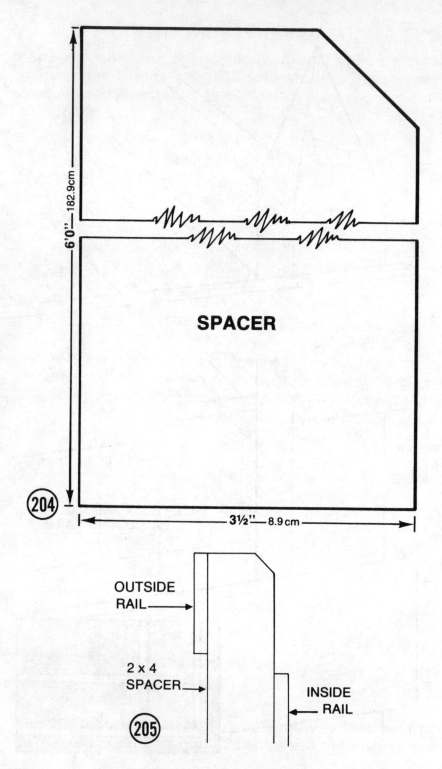

SPACER

6'0"—182.9 cm

3½"—8.9 cm

204

OUTSIDE RAIL

2 x 4 SPACER

INSIDE RAIL

205

FACTS ABOUT GLAZING WINDOWS

Glass in a wood frame is usually held in place with triangular glazier points and putty, Illus. 206, or a wood molding called a glass bead or putty bead. Never replace glazier points in the same holes.

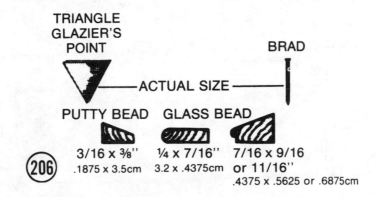

TRIANGLE GLAZIER'S POINT

BRAD

— ACTUAL SIZE —

PUTTY BEAD	GLASS BEAD	
3/16 x 3/8"	1/4 x 7/16"	7/16 x 9/16
.1875 x 3.5cm	3.2 x .4375cm	or 11/16"
		.4375 x .5625 or .6875cm

(206)

Glass in steel frames is held with a wire clip, Illus. 207, and putty. The irregular shaped leg A presses against glass, the straight leg B snaps into a hole in frame, Illus. 208. Putty is then applied as in a wood window.

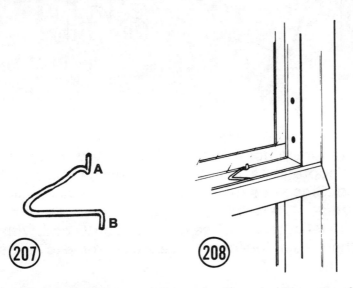

A

B

(207)   (208)

Some steel sashes were manufactured with a steel molding. This is screwed in the same position as a glass bead.

Aluminum window manufacturers used the kind of spring clip shown in Illus. 209. The shaped head fits under edge of glass, Illus. 210, 211, the legs are spread to butt against frame. Most glaziers use one close to the ends, one every 16 to 18''. The putty is then applied and beveled.

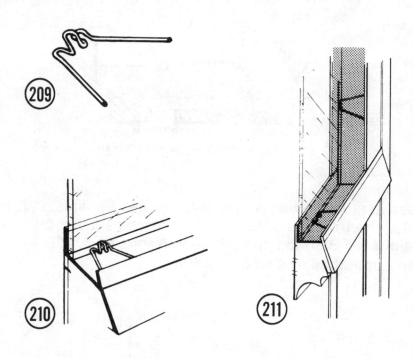

Some aluminum window manufacturers now set glass in a plastic or neoprene gasket, Illus. 212. This can be pried out and reused. Since this may be difficult to replace, use care not to damage it. Always use the same thickness glass as originally installed. Do not use putty, or a putty bed, with this gasket. When replacing, apply vaseline on frame to help slide gasket in place.

Always remove broken glass and inspect old putty for clips. Always note how many and where these clips were installed.

After removing broken glass, scrape frame carefully to remove bits of old putty. If putty is hard, apply heat using a torch or soldering iron. When area is clean, paint rabbet with linseed oil or paint primer. When dry, roll out a ribbon of putty and spread it thin over area receiving glass. Use a putty knife. This is called a "putty bed" and is important. It provides a cushion that seals out cold air, prevents windows from rattling, while it absorbs any irregularities in frame or glass. Many windows are manufactured without this bed.

Don't spread the putty bed too thick. This creates globs. Spread only as much putty as the frame requires to provide a smooth base, Illus. 213. Apply a putty bed to all frames except those that contain a preformed plastic or neoprene gasket.

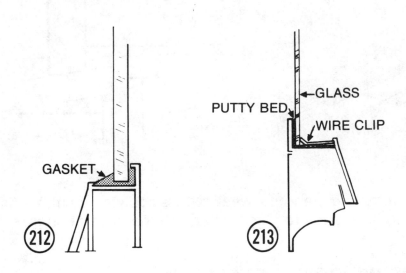

Always cut glass to size of opening, less ⅛" in overall width and height. This provides 1/16" clearance all around. If you have no confidence in your ability to measure the glass area, cut a cardboard pattern full size of opening less ⅛". Note how pattern fits into opening with just 1/16" clearance all around. Ask your glass retailer to match the pattern. Tell him you have already allowed for ⅛" clearance and he'll consider you a pro.

WOOD WINDOW — PUTTY

Press glass into putty bed. Use edge of chisel or screwdriver to press or tap glazier points in frame about 2" from corners of a small window; and every 10" from corner in a larger window. Glazier points need only be driven in about ½ their overall height. Use care not to scratch glass.

Knead putty to make it pliable, then roll it into long strips about pencil thickness. Place it in rabbet, press and bevel with a putty knife, Illus. 214. The linseed oil or paint primer permits putty to bond to frame.

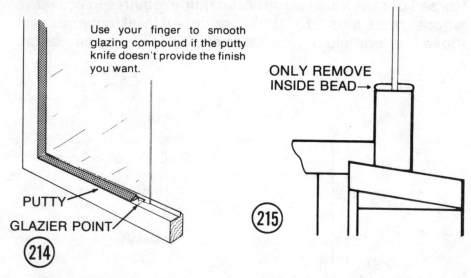

Use your finger to smooth glazing compound if the putty knife doesn't provide the finish you want.

ONLY REMOVE INSIDE BEAD→

PUTTY

GLAZIER POINT

(214)

(215)

Allow putty to dry about a week before applying paint. When painting, seal putty to glass with a hairline of paint on glass.

WOOD WINDOW — GLASS BEAD

Remove all broken glass. Glass bead is usually nailed in place with small brads. Note where bead was nailed and insert a wood chisel, wide screwdriver or narrow putty knife, in center, Illus. 215, preferably alongside a brad. Carefully raise bead, pull brads using pliers wherever nailed.

Carefully lift out inside bead at mitered corners. Never remove outside bead. Scrape away old paint and putty. Paint area with linseed oil. Spread a putty bed as outlined previously. Replace glass and renail bead along short sides first. Bow to insert longer lengths in position. Make new holes when renailing. Countersink heads of brads. Fill old and new nail holes with putty, then paint.

Because of warpage, or paint build up, the bead in many old frames is sometimes difficult to remove without damage. If damage occurs, repair with putty after replacing bead. Or install new glass bead. If the original glass was installed without a bed of putty, you will find it necessary to file ends of miter to shorten overall length. Always maintain angle of miter.

STEEL SASH

Replacing a window in a steel sash requires special clips, Illus. 207, 208. The broken glass and old putty is removed. It's frequently necessary to use a propane torch to loosen old putty on a metal sash. Again apply a thin bed of putty before setting glass in place. Press one leg of spring clip against glass, the other leg snaps into predrilled holes in sash, Illus. 208. Putty is then applied as previously described.

If steel sash has metal glass beads, these are screwed to frame. Spray screws with Liquid Wrench, insert screwdriver in screw slot, hit screwdriver lightly with hammer. This frequently jars screws loose.

ALUMINUM WINDOWS

Glass in these windows is held in place with clips, Illus. 209, and putty. Again remove glass and putty. Apply putty bed and replace glass. Press clips into place. Place head under edge while legs press against frame. Bevel putty to width frame requires.

Always purchase double strength glass for larger windows, single strength for smaller windows. If you have one window that gets broken more than usual, consider Plexiglas or acrylic. While it costs more, it lasts much, much longer.

REPAIRING LAWN FURNITURE

The horizontal courses of plastic chair webbing is usually applied first, Illus. 216. This will either be tacked to the side or underside on wood frame chairs, Illus. 217; or fastened to aluminum tubing with a ⅝" aluminum edging, Illus. 218. The edging acts as a clamp to hold webbing in position.

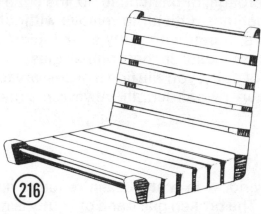

(216)

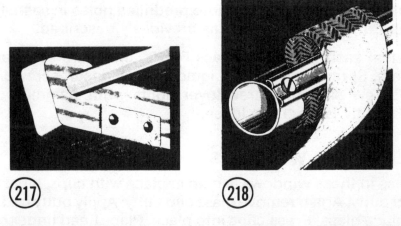

(217)   (218)

½" aluminum panhead tapping screws hold webbing clamp to tubing. If edging is riveted, drill through center of rivit and remove rivet. You can refasten clamp with aluminum panhead screws.

Cut webbing to length of piece removed and reweave following the original design, Illus. 219, 220.

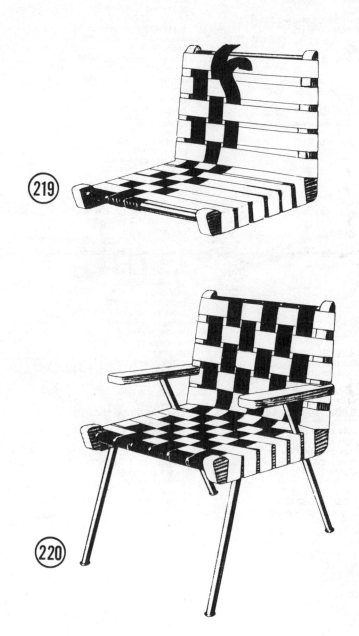

INDEX TO MONEY-SAVING REPAIRS, IMPROVEMENTS, PATTERNS AND BOOKS

(Number designates EASI-BILD Pattern or Book)

Acoustic Ceiling 615,665,685
Add-a-Room 609
Adhesives,use of 623, ceramic tile 606
Air Cooler, window 135
Air Conditioner,framing 632,665,685,773
Airplane,see toy
Alarm,devices 695
   bell , fire
   automatic telephone alarm
Anchor bolts 84,609,617,663,697
Antiquing 623,761
Apron,window 605,609,679,685
Asphalt Roofing 696
Asphalt Tile,how to lay 615,665
Attic Modernization 665,603,773
   built-in lighting 694
Baby Cradle 761
Ballcock,toilet 675
Bars 690
   buffet 718
   cabinet 189,690
   colonial tavern 612
   corner 690
   playroom 490,690
   radio & Hi-Fi 490
   revolving shelf 508
   room divider 658
   sink 490
   storage 634
   table 140
   TV bar 690
   wall 612
   wine storage 634
Barbecue 73,316,668
Barge boat 77
Batter boards 609,631,632,663,679,680
Basement,house 632
Basement Modernization 615
   drapery 627; electrical wiring 694
   entry 615; luminous ceilings 694
   waterproofing 617
Baseboard 605,609; radiation 685
Bathroom Accessories
   bathtub beauty bar 327
   bathtub repairs 675,682
   lavatory enclosure 158,606
   medicine chest repairs 694
   radiator enclosure 544
   shelf 4,5,8,557
   towel rack 29; vanity 606
Bathroom Installation 682,685
   bathtub,lavatory,medicine cabinet
   plumbing wall
   prefab bathroom unit, shower, toilet
Beds and Bunks
   colonial string bed 68,761
   double-deck 87,771
   headboard 126
   houseboat 676
   studio 633,623
   under bed storage 634
Bell alarm 695
   installation 694
Benches
   cobbler's 102A,586,761
   colonial 23,94,309,586
   dining 307; fireside 23,761
   lawn 57,325,307; peasant 57
   work 15,568,576,672,677
Bi Fold Door, closet 634

Birdhouses, feeders 669
   bluebird 110,669
   feeder 9,669,677
   martin 669; Swedish 10
   wrens 11,111,669,756
Blackboard
   kitchen message center 313,578
   play table 117,771
Bluebird house 110,669
Boats
   barge or pram 77
   cartop float 247
   houseboat 676
   kayak 317,757
   rowboat 77,85
   sail,centerboard 194
   sail scooter 248
   surfboard 247
   toy 60,67,72,771
Body harness 674,696,773
Bolts, anchor, see anchor bolts
Bookcases 664,658,634,690
   desk 18; hanging 21
   record comb. 192
   room divider 658; valance 271
   wall-to-wall 612,658,664,719
   window 271
Bookends 102A,756
Bow window 609
Breezeway
   how to build 910
   how to screen 613,781
Bricklaying 668,674
   walls, walks, terraces,
   veneering, mortar mixes
Bridging 609,613,697
Broomcloset 156,634
Buildings, see Garage,Homes,Houses
Built-In
   bookcase 664
   closet 634
   counter range 608,658
   cornice 605,627
   hi-fi 612
   lighting 694
   record storage 192,436,612,634,658
   refrigerator 608,658
   sewing center 634
   sink 608,658
   storage units 634
   traverse track 627
   wall oven 608,658
   wall-to-wall 612,634,664
Buffet, bar 718
   dining 138,718
Bulletin Board 93,607
Bungalow, see cabins
Bunks, see beds
Burglary alarm installation 695

Cabinets
   bar 189,690
   built-in 658; cleaning utensil 156
   contemporary 658; corner 38
   display 159M,607,627; end table 141
   fishing rod 130,630;freestanding 658
   furniture 658,634; gun 130,266,630
   hi-fi 272,612
   kitchen 201,242,243,244.
         245,246,608,658
   pole 658; record 192,436.612,658

trainboard 190,677
wall hanging 24; wall oven 608,658
wall-to-wall 191,192,193,608,
      634,658,664,719
wine storage 608,634
Cabins, cottages 51,84,91,632,684
Camper 594
Cane Webbing 623,757
Caning 623,757
Canopy 305,607
Canned goods storage 770,608,634
Canvas Deck 613,781
Cape Cod House 514
Carpeting 683
Carport 273,680,781
Casement window 609,613,781
Casing 609,605
Cat entry 724,751
Caulking also calking 613,682
Cavy Cage 751
Cedar Room 265,634
Ceiling joists 609,613,615,632
Ceiling,suspended 615,665,685
Ceiling trim plate 674
Ceramic tile, how to lay 606
Chairs
   child's lawn 132,754
   interior 92,306
   lawn 32,56,169,311,322R,548,754
   repair 623; refinish 623
   reupholstery 623
Chaise 78,169,312,324R,754
Chalk line 617,697
Charts, reference; drill bits 76l,753
   glue 623
   kitchen equipment 608
   lumber conversion—lineal ft.
     to board ft. 623
   metric conversion 606,607,677,751,761
   molding 623
   nails 634,627; screws 623,658
Chest,see wardrobe
   blanket 37,761,962
   cabinet 129
   storage 634
   tool 71,576,672
   toy and storage 37,65,962,771
   wardrobe 723,771
Chicken house 14
Children's Furniture
   blackboard,message center 313,578
   blackboard table 117,771
   bookcases & shelves 18,21,192,664
   book ends 102A,756; bulletin board 93
   bunks and beds 68,87,771
   desk 18,537; door stops 102B
   giraffe clothes tree 34,771
   headboard 126; lawn chair 132
   lamps 98; magazine rack 25,920
   picture frames 97; playtable 117,771
   record and hi-fi cabinets 192,272,436
   shoe shine box 45; shoe rack 345
   step stool 353,771
   storage cabinets 138,634
   storage chest 37,65,962
   telephone shelf 313
   TV tables 16,925
   trainboard 190,677
   wall decorations 539,580,581,756
   wall shelves 4,6,31,35,159M,578

Child's Playhouse 148,649
Chimes, Swedish door 561,677
Chimney 91,910,674,696
   construction 674
   cricket 674,696
   flashing 674,696
   flat roof 674
   prefabricated 632 ,685
   slip section 674
Christmas Displays
   angel 769
   angel banner 670
   animated 762,764
   camels 410C
   candy cane 435
   carolers 331
   choir boys 562
   fireplace mantel 768
   giant cards, posters, murals
     149,331,540,560,562,592,
     762,764,769,942A,942B
   illuminated 560,562,592,764,767,769,694
   indoor decorations 310,767,768
   madonna 149,540,767
   nativity 310(table top)
          410(life size)
   noel greeting 531
   reindeer & sleigh 433,434,764
   santa 431,575,762
Christmas Displays
   window painting 149
   wise men greeting 560
   wreath 767
Cistern, how to build 617
Clamps 623
Clapboard, siding 609,613,631
Closets 634,773
Clothes Tree 34,771
Clothing storage 634,771
Cobbler's bench 102A,586,761
Coffee tables, see table
Colonial
   bench 23,761; cabinet 627
   candleholder 559
   cobblers bench 102A,586,761
   corner cupboard 38
   cradle-rocker 753, 773; cupola 589
   doll cradle 753, 773; furniture 761
   hutch cabinet 270,761
   planters 102A,933,756,761
   table-bench 94,761
   tavern bar 612
   wall shelves 2,24; weathervane 524
   window valance 1,27,30,157,627
Concrete & Masonry
   barbecue 73,316,668,674
   bricklaying 668,674
   chimney 674
   block layout stick 617
   colors 617
   culverts, curbs 732
   decorator blocks 582
   floors, garage & basement 273,615,617
     632,663,680,697
   footprint stepping stones 96
   foundations & footings 84,86,113,
     609,613,617,632,663,697,781
   how-to-book 617
   mixing 617

Concrete & Masonry
  patio floor 591,631,606,781
  piles 567
  repairs 617
  steps 617,685
  tools 617
  waterproofing 617
  work simplified 617
Contemporary Furniture 658
Cooler, attic air 135
Cornice
  how to build 605,612,627
  install traverse rod 627
Corner cabinet 38,242,761
Cottages, see homes
Counter
  serving 80,243
  sink ,tops 608,658,685
Cradle, baby 761, 773
Cricket 696
Cupola, colonial 589.609,680
Day Bed, 633,623
Deck 631,763,773,781
Desks 18,139,537,542,608,658
Diagonal bracing 609,613,632
Dining, bench 307
  buffet 138
  table 94,95,137,554
Displays, see Christmas displays
  case 159M,607
Dividers, room 128,263,308,605,
    608,658,930
  outdoor privacy 607,617,631,668,937
Dog House 28,751
Doll carriage 59,61
  cradle 753, 773
Dollhouse 33,596,753; furniture 753
Door
  bi-fold 634
  chimes 561,677
  decorate with plysculpture 704
  dutch 649,679
  garage 86; swing-up 763
  glass sliding 613,781
  hayloft 679
  how to install 608,609,613,615,631,658
  modernizing 623
  remove 608
  outside entry 615
  sliding 658,679,680
  storage 634
Dormer,how to build 603,665,773
Double hung windows 609,613,685
Drain, clogged 675
Drainage Tile 617,615
Drapery 627
  how to make 627
  traverse track installation 627,605
Drawers
  how to build 608,658
Driveway
  culverts, curbs 732
  markers 438,587
Dry Well 617
Easel, artists 555
Edging Tool
  concrete 617
Electric Light Gardening 611,694
Electrical Repairs 694
  wiring, built-in lighting 694

End tables 99,127,141,925
Enclosures
  books, see built-in
  brooms, mops 156,634
  chimney 674
  hi-fi and record 192,272,436.612
  lavatory 158,606
  lighting 694; porch 613,781
  pots and pans 578; radiator 544
  refrigerator 608,658
  sink 41,158; trains 190,677
  truck body camper 594
  wall oven 608,658
  window, see valance
Entry, outdoors 615,617
Excavating 663
Expansion joint 613
Expansion plug 613,615,631,658,781
Express wagon 40
Exterior Siding 609,663,696,763
Fan, window 135
Farmyard animals 79,83,771
Fascia 609,613,632,663,696,781
Faucet
  repairs 675
  replacement 675
  seat 675
Feeders, bird 9,669
Fences 668,607
  rail 941,607
  privacy 937,607,668,781
  Williamsburg 315,607
Ferrule 682,696
Fireplace 73,316,668,674
  Christmas 768
  freestanding 674
  gas 674
  hot air circulating 674
  indoor 674
  mantel 231,605,674
  masonry 674
  open end 674
  outdoor 73,316,668
  radiant heat 674
Firestop 674
Fishing gear
  storage 130,266,630
Flashing 603,609,613,665,696
  chimney 674
Float,cartop swimming 247
Floating concrete 613,617,781
Floodlights 694,695
Floor
  how to lay 615,665
  level 608,685
  repair 608,685
  tile 606
  underlay 615
Flush Valve, toilet 675
Foam rubber, upholstery 623
Folding
  chair 56; settee 55
  snack table 43
Footing 113,609,613,615,
    617,663,697,781
Footprints, giant 96
Form 613,617,668,697
Foundations 609,613,617,632.
    668,697,781
  waterproofing 632

Frames, picture 623,702
  window 159,605
Framing roof,floor,walls, new openings
  501,502,603,609,613,631,632,
  685,696,697,910,781
Free standing room divider 658
Furniture
  cabinet 634,658
  colonial 761
  contemporary 658
  dollhouse 753
Furniture, repair 623
  antiquing 623,761; caning 623
  cane webbing 623,757
  spring replacement 623
  refinishing 623; reupholstery 623
Furring 609,605,615
Gable roof, studs 609,696,697
Gambrel 679
Garage
  doors, overhead 86; swing-up 763
  one car 680
  transform into housing 684
  two car 663
  two car/apartment above 763
Garden, hotbed 611
  tool house 51,89,649
  trellis 304
Gates 315,941,607
Girders, covering 615,605
Glass sliding doors 613,763,781
Glazing 623,781
Glider, lawn 155,754
Gluing, complete guide 623
  furniture 623
Golf cart 583
Grade level, establishing 632,668
Greenhouse 112,566,571,611
Grill, stall door 680,679
Grout 606,617,613,668,781
Guest house 84,684
Guide lines, laying out 632,668,697
Gun
  cabinets 130,266,630
  racks 574,630
Gutter 609,631,632,696,781
Gymnasium, outdoor 152,153,154

Hamster Cage751
Hardware
  drapery 605, garage door 86
Headboard 126
Header 608,609,613,632,696,668,781
Hearth, prefabricated 674
Hi-Fi and radio 272,612
Hobby Horse 54,771
Home Workshop 677
Homes
  country cottage 91
  five-bedroom Cape Cod 514
  guesthouse 84
  hillside 103H—plans only
  southwest corner 432,632
  three-bedroom modern 502,513
  three-bedroom ranch 501
  two story garage apartment 763
  two-bedroom ranch 910
  valley house 103V—plans only
Hotbed, garden 611
Houseboat 676—26´; pontoons 600

House numbers, signs 801,607
Houses
  retirement 632; bird 669
  dog 28,751; doll 33,596,753
  duck-in 725,751;
  garden tools 51,89,649
  green or hothouse 112,571; hog 13
  lean-to storage 89,649; martin 669
  play 148,649; poultry 14
  rehabilitate 685; wiring 694
Hunter's cabinet 266,630
Hutch cabinet 270,761
  rabbit 751
Indirect Lighting 694
Indoor Fireplace 674,231
Iron railings, repair 685

Jamb 605,697
Jig Saw, Pattern Asst. 102A
  with 10 full-size patterns 756

Kayak 317,757
Kitchen
  blackboard 578
  broom closet 156,634
  buffet 138
  cabinets 201,241-2-3-4-5-246,
    608,658,634
  counters 80,201,244,245,608,658
  equipment templates 608,658
  knife rack 8; lighting 694
  modernizing 605,608,685
  planning 608; range installation 608
  serving counter 80,243
  sink enclosure 41,158
  sink trap 682; traverse track 627
  unit 3; utility closet 156
  wall shelves 2,4,5,8
  wall oven 608,658
  work bench 573
Kite, Bermuda 314,771
Knick-Knack, see shelves

Lamps
  modern table 98
  outdoor colonial post 935,607
  planter 541
  repair 694
  rooster, pin up 533
  shadow box 557,301
Land selection 632
Lavatory enclosure 158,606
  P trap 682
  repair 675
Lawn or Patio
  bench 57,307,325
  chairs 32/39,55/56,311,314,
    322R,548,754
  chaise 78,169,312,324R,754
  furniture repairs 623
  glider 155,754
  ornaments 9,81,96,304,102A,672.756
  settee 39,55
  tables 17,22,75,323,554,577,754
Layout Stick
  brick 668
  concrete block 617
  clapboard siding 609,684
  tile 606
Lazy Susan 608,677
Lean-to tool shed 89,649,kennel,751
Level-Transit 668,697,763

INDEX TO MONEY-SAVING REPAIRS, IMPROVEMENTS, PATTERNS AND BOOKS

Lighting 694
  built-in cornice,valance 605,694
  dark corner 557
  living room, draperies 627,694
  luminous ceiling, luminous 615,694
  wall sconce, candle 559
  walls, soffits, cove 694
Louver
  how to install 665,632,773
Lumber,chart 623
Magazine, rack 25,920,658,761
Mantel, fireplace 231,605,674
Martin House 669
Medicine Chest, repair 694
Message center, blackboard 313,578
Metal repairs
  roofing 696
Miter joint 605,609,664
Modern furniture 658
  also see furniture,bookcase,table
Modernization, attic 665,603,665,773
  bathroom 606,682
  basement 605,615
  kitchen 608,658,685
  lighting 694
  metal and wood cabinets 608,605
  refrigerator 605,608
Mortar—how to mix 668,617
  apply 609,613,617
Mullion or munion 613,609
Music Wall 612

Name Plates,Signs 438,587,801,607
Night tables 343

Ornaments
  Christmas, see subject
  door chimes 561,677
  driveway 438
  sign & nameplate 801,607
  table top 46; wall-hanging 301,539,
  559,580,581,102,756
Outbuildings, see houses
Outdoor, lighting 694
Outlets, Electrical 694

Paneling,how to apply 605,609,615,665
Parakeet cage, 751
Partitions, see dividers 608,605,615
  658,665,773
Partition footings 632; post 617
  stable 679,680
  wall 501,502
Patio
  bench 57
  furniture, see lawn
  how to build 617,631,668,781
  how to screen 631,781
  paver tile 606,617,781
Peasant, shelf 2,4
  table 17
Pet projects
  cat shelter 724,751
  dog house 28,751
  dog kennel 751
  duck or chick-inn 725,751
  pet housing 751
  parakeet cage 751
  rabbit hutch 751
Picnic, see tables
Picture frames 97,623,702
Pipe rack, smoking 49,630

Pipes, covering 615
  repair 675
Pitch of roof 609,613,696,697,781
Planters
  indoors 46,82,102A,761,756
  lamp 541
Plaque, child's wall 102A,756
Plastic Laminate
  how to apply 608,658
  panels 631
Playground equipment
  see toys
Playhouses 148,649
Playroom bar 189,490,690,634
Play table 117,771
Plumb, how to 609,613,617,
  632,668,773
Plumbing 675
  continuous waste 682
  drain 682
  drum trap 682
  ferrule 682,696
  fittings 682
  fresh air inlet 682
  horizontal branch 682
  increaser 682
  kitchen sink trap 682
  lavatory 682
  plumbing wall 682
  repairs 675
  revent 682
  rough in 675,682
  slip joint 682
  soil pipe 682
  solder cup end 682
  spigot 682
  stack 682
  stack vent 682
  wall frame 632
  water pipe riser
Plunger
  toilet 675
Plywood
  how to panel 605
Pontoon 676,600
Pony
  book ends 102A,756
  rocker 53,771
Porch
  add-on 567,631,781
  build 613,781
  enclose 613,781
  sliding glass doors 613,781
Potholders Holder 756
Pram 77
Privacy partition 607,631,668,781
Quarry Tile
  606,617
Rabbit Hutch 751
Rack
  gun 630
  towel 29
Radio and Stereo
  bar 690
  cabinets 612,272
  how to build-in 612
Radiator enclosure 544,677
Rafters 609,613,631,632,663,679,696,781
Range installation 608
Record Cabinets 192,436,612

144

Refrigerator
  enclosure 608,658
  modernization 608,605
Reinforcing Rods, wire 617,668
Relax-a-Board 161
Remodeling 609,685,781
Repairs
  cane webbing 623,757
  concrete 617
  electrical 694
  furniture 623
  picture framing 623
  plumbing 675
  roofing 696
  tile 606
Ridge shingles 696
Rocker, pony ride 53,771
Rod, traverse 627
Roofing Repairs
  and Application 696
  asphalt
  repairs
  roll roofing
  safety harness 674,696,773,781
  scaffold 665,668,696
  slate; wood
Room, add on 609,760
  dividers 128,658
  furniture 658
  roughing in 682
  wiring 694
Rowboats 77,85
Rush Weaving 623

Sabre Saw Pattern
  10 full-size projects 102A,756,672
Safety, see signs
Safety harness 696
Sailboat 194,248
Sandbox 20,77
Sawhorse-chest 672
Scaffold 665,668,679,680,696
Sconce, candle wall 559
Screed 617,631
Screen Enclosure 613,631
  how to make 631,781
Screw chart 658
Second floor apartment 763,773
Septic Tank 675
Service, center 243; counter 80
Settee, see Lawn
Sewer Line 675
Sewing Cabinet 634
Sewing Tables 543
Shadow box 301,557
Sheathing, exterior 609,613,663,679,696
Shelves, wall 2,4,5,6,8,21,24,634,
  658,672,605
Shim 609,605
Shingles, asbestos 113,696,910
  roofing 432,609,663,696,910
Shoe rack 345
Shoe shine box 45
Shoe Equipment; see workbench
Siding installation 609,663,696
Signs, nameplates 801,607
Sink, repairs 675
  bar 201,608,658,690
  counter installation 608
  enclosure 41,158,606

Skylight, how to install 665,696,773
Slant board 161
Slate Roofing 696
Slides, child's 63
Sliding door, wardrobes 139,634,658,773
Sliding stable door 679,680
Soil pipe 675,682
Solar heated greenhouse 611
Springs, furniture, cord bed 623
  retying, replacing, no-sag 623
Stable 679,680
Stairs, concrete 615,617
  how to build 603,615,617,665
    outside 763,781
Stall door 679,680
Star drill 679,680
Step Flashing 603,609,696
Stereo Wall 612
Stool, Tot's Step 353,771
Stilts 552,771
Stool, sill 605
Storage
  cabinets 3,24,159,634,242,608,658
  canned goods 770,608,623
  chest 37,962,634,771
  doll 159M
  garden tool house 649
  headboard 126
  room divider 658
  sewing 634
  underbed 37,634,761
  undersink 41,158
  understair 634
  walls 612,658,634
  walls on casters 263
  wine storage 608,634,690
Storm windows 303
Stringer stair 603,665,763,773
Structural lighting 694
Studs 761,910,603
Studio bed, string 633,623,761
Subflooring 609
Sump Pump 615,617
Sundeck 631,763,773,781
Sunhouse 611
Surfboard or swimming float 247
Suspended ceiling 615
Swimming pool enclosure 631,781
Swings 152,155,754
Switch, wall 605,694

Tables
  bar 140, bridge 95, child's 117,771
  coffee 52,140,309,326,452
  colonial 94,761
  dining 94,95,137,554
  end 99,127,141
  folding 94,323,754
  lawn or terrace 17,75,326,554,754
  night table 343
  picnic 17,22,323,577,754
  round top 75,326,754
  serving, see coffee
  sewing 543
  TV 16,925
  wall attached 26,774
  workshop 15,568,573,576,672
Tape recorder, built-in 612
Telephone shelf 313
Termite Shield 609,632

Terrace 631,668,781
  table 75,326,754
Tile, see Ceramic 606
  asphalt 615
  counter 606
  how to lay 615
  vinyl 615
Toilet
  chemical, propane, jet 685
  installation 682, repairs 675
  replacement 675
Tool chests 71,576,634,672
Tommy gun, see toys
Tool houses
  expandable 51
  garage 113
  garden 51,649
  lean-to 89,649
  red barn 679
Tourist house 84,684
Towel rack 29
Toys
  airplane 70
  animals 79,83,771
  artists easel 555; boats 60,67,771
  carriage 59,753,773; chest 634
  circus group 48,771
  climbing, see playground
  clown 47,771; dollhouse 33,596,753
  furniture, see Children's
  dollhouse 753
  gas cart 583; glider 70
  gym, see playground
  hobby horse 54,771; machine gun 62
  how to build 771
  playground equipment
    climbing pole 154
    complete gym 152
    merry-go-round 733
    monkey bar 153
    sandbox 20,77
    slide 63
  playhouse 148,649
  playtable 117,771
  pony rocker 53,771; repairs 623
  stable 679
  step-stool 353,771; stilts 552,771
  storage 634,65; tommy gun 58
  toy chest 65,771; trainboard 190,677
  wagon 40; wheelbarrow 66
  workbench 15,672
Trainboard 190,677
Trap 675,682
  bathtub
  drum
  lavatory
  sink
  waste line
Traverse track 627
Tree bench 617
Tree well 668
Trellis 305
Trim, apply 615
Trophy cabinet 630,792
Truss clips 679,697
TV table 16
Under bed storage 634,761
Understair storage 634
Upholstery, repair 623
Utility closet 156,634

Valance
  bookcase 271
  indirect lighting 157,694
  window 1,27,30,550,627
Valley Flashing 696,773
Vanity 658
  bathroom 606
Veneer, brick 668

Wall decorations 97,159M,539,
    580,581,702, see ornaments
Wall
  framing 663,608
  oven 608,658
  paneling 605
  plaque, child's 102A,756
  remove 608,685
  retaining 668
  shelves, see shelves
  storage 634,761
  switch 694
  waterproof 615
  wiring 694
Walks, brick 668
Wardrobe 139,193,263,634,658
Washers
  faucet 675
  sizes 675
Water pipe riser 682
Water Shut Off
  valve 675
Waterproofing 617
Weathervane 524,588,589
Webbing, furniture 623
Wheelbarrow 66
Wind braces 632
Window
  bookcase 271
  bow, picture, installation 609
  framing 159,605
  glazing 613,623,781
  greenhouse 566,611
  how to install 609
  how to move 608
  how to repair window 685,773
  storm 303
  valance 1,27,30,550,605,627,694
Wiring, electric 615,694
Wood conversion chart 613
Wood shingles 696
Workbench 568,672,677
Workshop 677
Worktable 573,672
Wren house 11,111,756